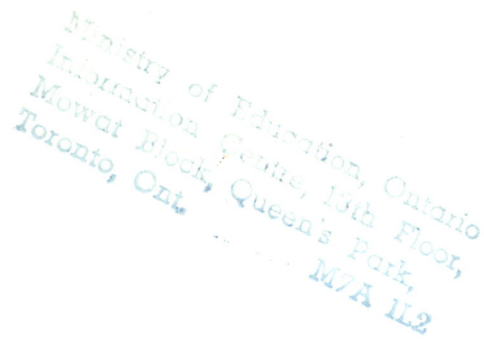

SWITCHED OFF:

THE SCIENCE EDUCATION OF GIRLS

Jan Harding

LONGMAN FOR SCHOOLS COUNCIL

1983

Published by Longman for Schools Council
Longman Resources Unit
33-35 Tanner Row
York YO1 1JP

Copyright © 1983
Schools Council Publications

CONTENTS

	Foreword	page	5
1	Introduction		7
2	The position in the seventies		8
3	Illuminating the problem		17
4	What action can we take?		36
	References		50
	Further reading		57

FOREWORD

This pamphlet is the direct result of a joint venture between the Schools Council and the Equal Opportunities Commission. The Schools Council is charged with developing the school curriculum, the EOC with the promotion of sex equality; in 1979 they decided to pool their expertise in these areas and to collaborate in a series of pamphlets on sex differentiation in a range of curricular areas.

The Schools Council has affirmed its commitment to equal educational opportunities for girls and boys. It has set up a Sex Differentiation in Schools Working Party and has funded a range of activities aimed at reducing sex bias in education. The issue of sex differentiation is increasingly recognised as important. Research continues to demonstrate the sexual inequality of our educational provision and many educationists are actively involved in developing ways of reducing the disadvantage experienced by boys and girls.

Science is an area in which girls have long experienced such disadvantage. Alison Kelly estimated that 85 per cent of girls leave school with only a minimal knowledge of physical sciences. At every level in the education system, females are under-represented in science compared with males. For a variety of reasons girls appear reluctant to tackle the physical sciences yet, though so few are attracted, there is no evidence that girls are less able than boys.

In a receding employment market girls are likely to be particularly vulnerable where they lack education in subjects such as science and mathematics; these are essential to employment and training at a skilled level in the industrial, technological and engineering sectors. Moreover physical science provides pupils with the opportunity to build up confidence and familiarity with day to day technology. Thus women through the imbalance of their educational experience are unable to realise a variety of opportunities in career and personal terms. Furthermore, as an industrial nation, Britain's success is dependent on having a highly skilled scientific workforce. This in turn is dependent on being able to draw on the skills and talents of the whole of the population.

Jan Harding's scholarly pamphlet analyses the nature of the problem. She considers recent educational developments, explores relevant research findings, discusses the subtle ways in which stereotyping operates and presents a careful and considered case for re-thinking our attitudes to the scientific education of girls. To facilitate this she presents a range of strategies that schools can draw on to extend and promote girls' opportunities in science. Jan Harding has been particularly active in this area and her work at Chelsea College on science and girls has been widely acclaimed. We are most fortunate in being able to draw on this experience and expertise in a pamphlet which all those involved in the education of young people, not only scientists, will find illuminating and compelling.

LESLEY KANT
Schools Council

1. INTRODUCTION

Concern for girls' science education first found public expression in the 1960s, when the expansion of science in the universities and polytechnics failed to result in the anticipated increase in student applications. The Dainton Report in 1968[1] referred to the 'untapped pool of ability' in science amongst the female population. Since then sporadic attempts have been made to persuade girls to choose science and engineering courses. At the same time, other changes have taken place; the Nuffield Science Teaching Project materials[2] have variably influenced science courses, secondary schools have been reorganized from largely single-sex grammar and 'modern' schools to form mixed comprehensive schools, the school-leaving age has been raised to sixteen years and the Sex Discrimination Act has become law, accompanied by the setting up of the Equal Opportunities Commission.

How have these changes affected the involvement of girls in science? Department of Education and Science (DES) statistics, quoted in the press under the headline 'Girls switch to science', report large percentage increases in the numbers of girls taking chemistry and physics at O and A level (*Observer*, 1980). Is there still a cause for concern?

This pamphlet argues strongly that there is, and that there is considerable research and comment that we may draw upon to suggest strategies to increase girls' participation in the physical sciences and technology.

2. THE POSITION IN THE SEVENTIES

In order to assess whether the situation relating to girls and science is improving, it is important to look at trends over a period of years. Department of Education and Science statistics have been a useful source of data through which to monitor trends in entries to public examinations and degree courses, which will reflect the involvement of girls in science. The entry of new undergraduates to science and engineering courses in 1977 is shown in Figure 1. The strong bias to the male is still evident, especially in engineering where women form only 5 per cent of first-year students. This is, however, an increase of nearly 100 per cent over the 1973 figure of 2.7 per cent.

Entry to degree courses requires appropriate A-level qualifications; the trends in A-level entries over the 1970s are shown in Figures 2(a) and 2(b). The biggest differences between girls and boys are in mathematics and physics. Both of these subjects show an increased growth of entries (mathematics from 1975 and physics from 1977) for both girls and boys, but the actual increases involved are greater for the latter than for the former. This means that, whatever has caused the change, it has affected boys in greater numbers than it has girls, although percentage increases calculated for the girls may be more impressive because of the much lower starting figure.

Table 1 Destination of school-leavers with A-level passes in science and mathematics, 1978

	3 or more A levels Boys	3 or more A levels Girls	2 A levels Boys	2 A levels Girls
	%	%	%	%
Degree courses	83.4	78.2	53.7	31.5
Teacher training	0.2	0.3	–	1.4
Other further education	2.6	4.3	15.8	21.9
Employment	13.8	17.2	30.5	45.2
Total %	100	100	100	100
Total number	11,810	3,250	2,030	730

Source: Department of Education and Science. *Statistics of Education 1978*, vol.2 (HMSO, 1980).

In mathematics the sex differential is greater at A level, at 3.3 boys to 1 girl, than at undergraduate level, where it is 2.1:1, suggesting that a higher proportion of girls than boys with A-level mathematics qualifications enter mathematics degree courses. Many of the boys will use an A-level mathematics qualification to enter engineering courses. It seems that girls are not encouraged to regard mathematics as a service subject for a wide range of careers in the same way that boys are.

A smaller proportion of girls than boys with science and mathematics A levels enter degree courses, as Table 1 (p.8) shows. A higher proportion go directly into employment, indicating that the educational and vocational aspirations of these able girls are lower than those of the equivalent group of boys.

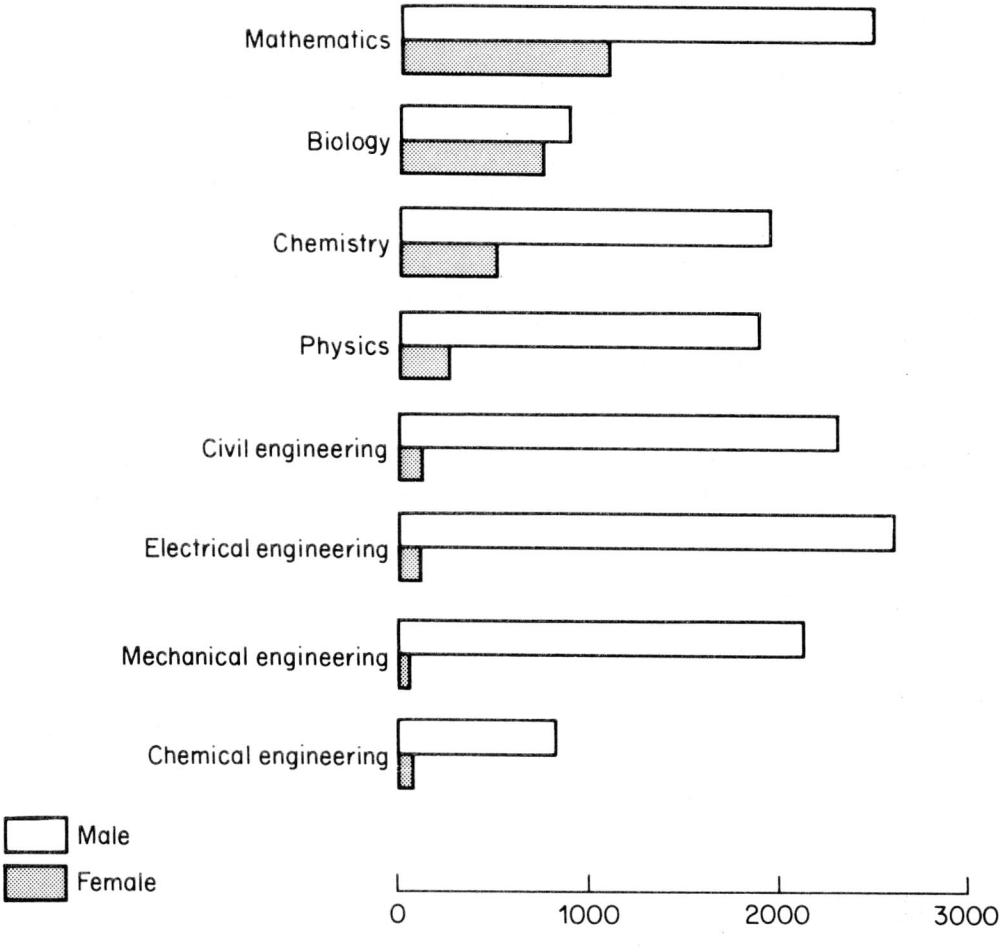

Figure 1 Full-time students at undergraduate level entered for the first time, 1977-78

Source: Department of Education and Science. *Statistics of Education 1977*, vol.6 (HMSO, 1980).

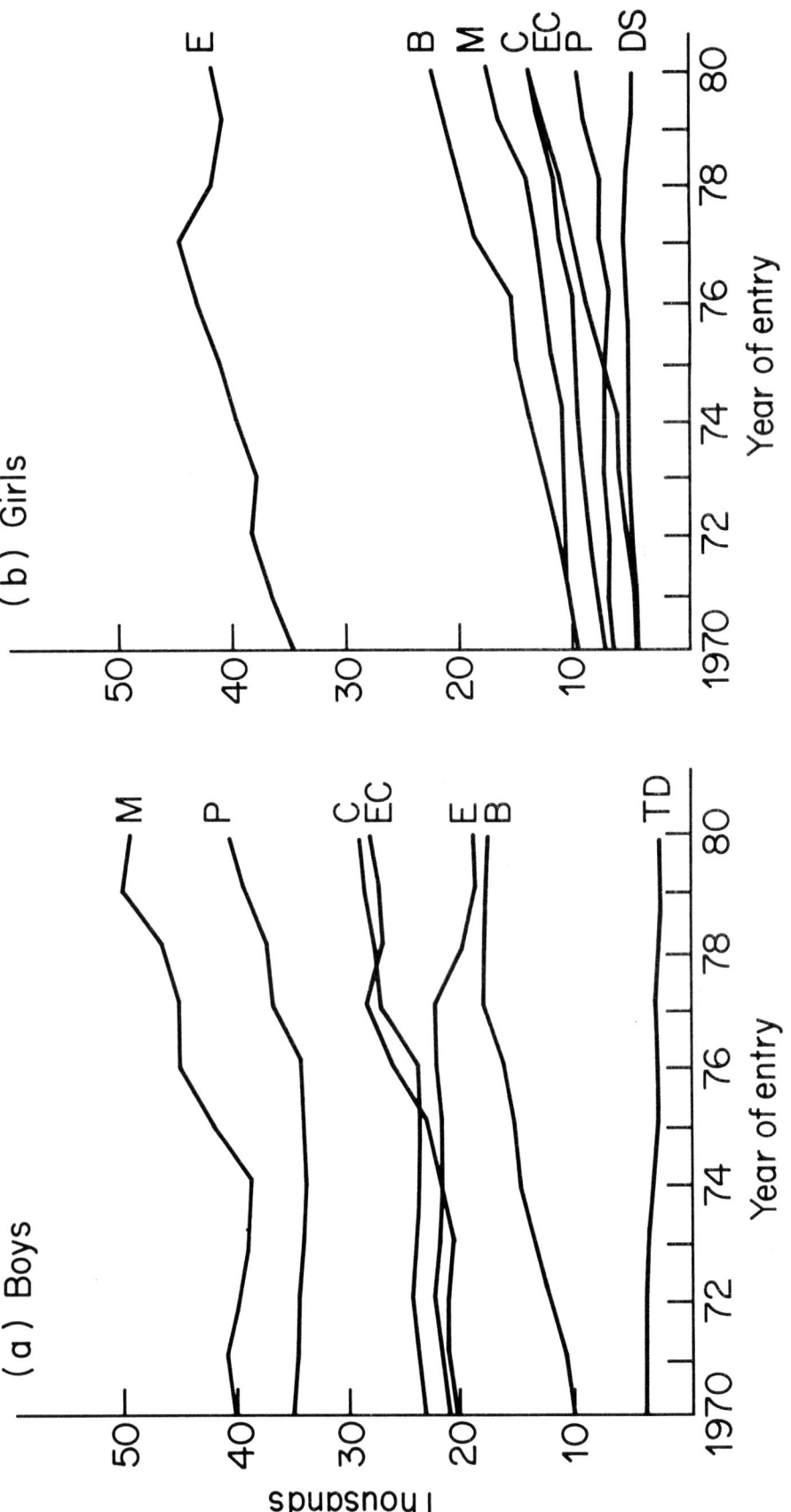

E = English; M = Mathematics; P = Physics; C = Chemistry; B = Biology; TD = Technical drawing; EC = Economics; DS = Domestic subjects

Figure 2   GCE A-level entries: summer 1970-80

Source: Department of Education and Science. *Statistics of Education*, vols.2, HMSO.

The 16+ entry figures represent the aspirations of some 90 per cent of the school population in 1980.* Figures 3(a) and 3(b) and 4(a) and 4(b) display the trends for O level and CSE over the 1970s. The increase in entries over the decade is partly, but not wholly, accounted for by the increase in school population which reached a maximum at 16+ in 1980.

The patterns for English language and mathematics are interesting. They are both core subjects in the curriculum but fewer candidates, both girls and boys, were entered for mathematics than for English. Does this imply a perceived greater difficulty of mathematics or its lesser importance in education? The 1980 entry for boys in mathematics shows a dramatic rise, to approach the figure for English language, but the girls' entry is still only just over half the English figure. A possible explanation for this is that public concern about mathematics education (expressed in the setting up of the Cockcroft Committee, for example, in 1979) has had a major influence on the expectation for boys, but affected girls very little.

In physics, the actual increase for boys, over the years represented, has been greater than for girls at both CSE and at O level, maintaining a ratio of just under four boys to one girl at O level and eight boys to one girl at CSE. Again, any increased resources in, or emphasis on, the physical sciences in the 11-16 curriculum has benefited boys more than girls, although the *percentage* increases for girls will be more impressive.† Technical drawing for girls only just appears on the CSE graph and does not even escape from the baseline at O level.

Science was one of the aspects of the curriculum included by HM Inspectors in the DES's secondary survey.[3] They found that 9 per cent of all boys and a disturbing 17 per cent of all girls followed no science course at all in the fourth and fifth years. Only 10 per cent of boys and 5 per cent of girls continued studying the three science subjects to 16+, while 60 per cent of girls and 50 per cent of boys chose only one science subject. This was usually biology for girls and physics for boys. Only some 12 per cent of all girls studied physics to 16+. Contrary to popular belief, general or combined science is used more by boys than by girls. Science in this form is clearly seen as more appropriate for the average and less able pupil than for the more able.

These data show that there can be little doubt that, while there has been a general increase in take-up of science subjects over the 1970s, this has featured boys rather more than girls. Why does this continued low participation by girls in the physical sciences cause concern?

---

* Although the combined CSE/GCE O-level examinations were originally intended to cater for the top 60 per cent only of a perceived ability range, DES statistics show that since the mid-70s a decreasing number of school-leavers have *not* attempted any public examination. In 1979 this reduced to 9 per cent.

† The 'switch to science' on the part of girls reported in the *Observer* newspaper (1980) arises from the almost zero increase in boys' entries in chemistry in the interval 1977/78 rather than from a noticeable change of pattern in girls' entries!

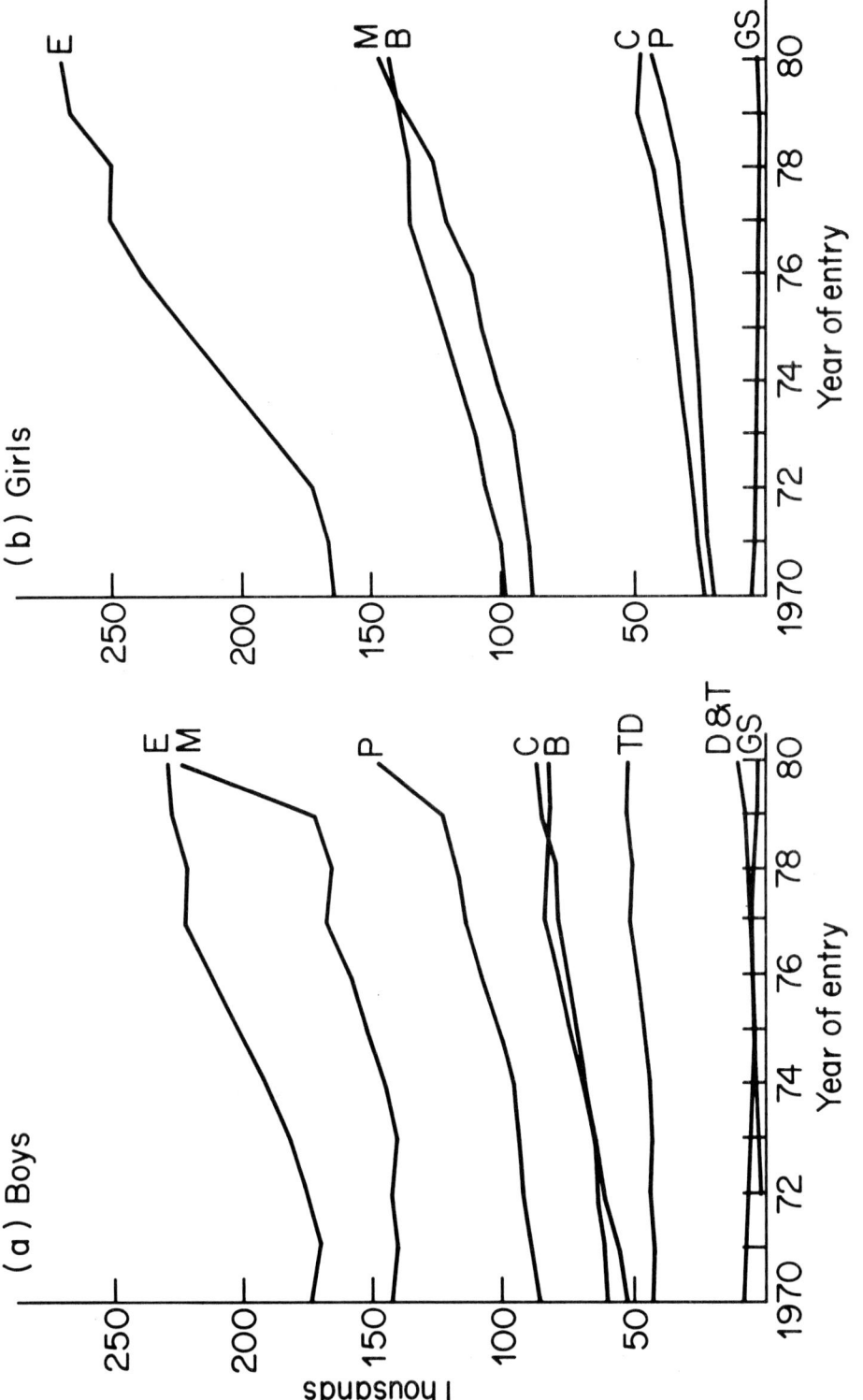

E = English; M = Mathematics; P = Physics; B = Biology; C = Chemistry; GS = General science; TD = Technical drawing; D&T = Design and technology

Figure 3 GCE O-level entries: summer 1970-80

Source: Department of Education and Science. *Statistics of Education*, vols.2, HMSO.

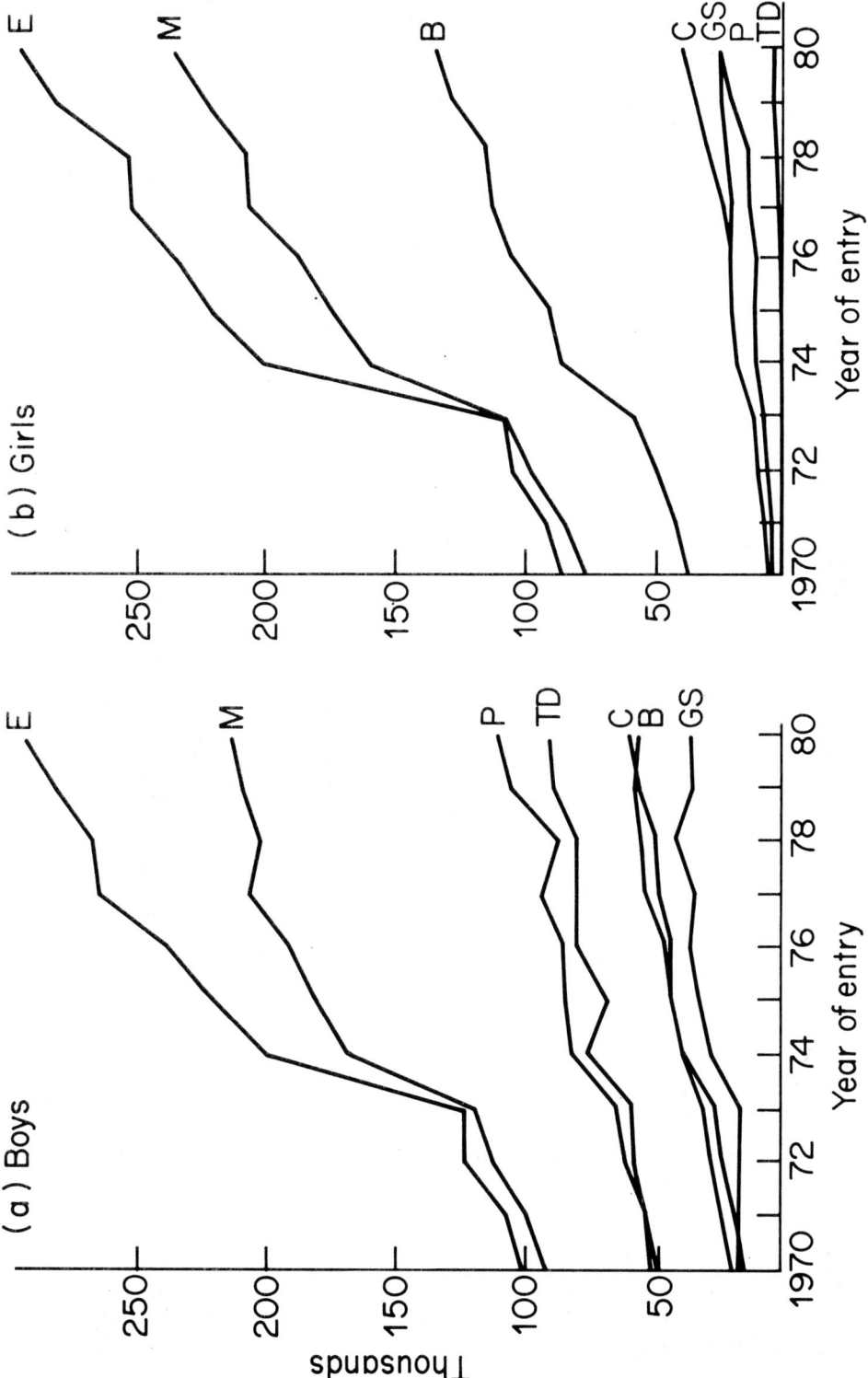

E = English; M = Mathematics; P = Physics; C = Chemistry; B = Biology; GS = General science; TD = Technical drawing

Figure 4   CSE entries: summer 1970-80

Source: Department of Education and Science. *Statistics of Education*, vols.2, HMSO.

Why we are concerned

In summing up their report on aspects of secondary education the HMI state:

> Close to the heart of any formulation of the aims of education must lie concern to develop the potential of all pupils to enjoy a full personal life and to take an informed and responsible part in the adult world, including their part in the economic life of the country. Curricular provision, therefore, ought not to be such as to shut off any pupils from important areas of knowledge and experience, or to suggest quite different views of their future role in society.[4]

But the small proportion of girls studying the physical sciences at school ensures that the representation of women in science-based work is limited and confirms the stereotyping of the physical sciences and technology as masculine activities. This, in turn, discourages even some able girls who are interested in these subjects from choosing to study them. So the girls are deprived of rewarding careers, and academic science and industry of able recruits. For girls in the middle range of ability (those currently attempting CSE examinations), these subjects are even more effectively stereotyped and many employment and training opportunities are closed to the majority who do not study the physical sciences. (E. Byrne demonstrates that over two-thirds of all further education courses, in part of the Midlands, required physical science and mathematics qualifications for entry.)[5]

Some question the importance of a career for women, however. Writing in the official mouthpiece of the DES, *Trends in Education*, after the passing of the Sex Discrimination Act in 1975, one HMI stated:

> We have decided that it is essential to ensure that boys and girls and men and women have equal access to educational opportunities. No country can risk leaving any mind undeveloped. And the children of a mother who is educated in the broadest sense are less likely to perpetuate low standards in their children. In our anxiety to be fair we need to recognise the plain fact that for most women home-making and bringing up children come first. For men the equivalent is to earn enough to support their wives and families.[6]

However, 'facts' collected and published by the Equal Opportunities Commission (EOC)[7] show that the 'labour force activity rate' (i.e. the number in, or seeking, employment) for all 16 to 59-year-old women was 72.6 per cent and 59.4 per cent for unmarried and married women, respectively, in 1979.* Moreover 54 per cent of mothers with children under 16 were working in 1980.

---

* For the General Household Survey preliminary data, the corresponding figures are 72 per cent and 62 per cent in 1980.[8]

The reasons for women seeking work are complex. For some it may be financial hardship, but work may serve other roles than earning a living. The fifth form girls surveyed by I. Rauta and A. Hunt certainly thought so. When asked to respond to the statement 'if I didn't need the money I wouldn't go out to work at all', 47 per cent rejected it completely and a further 31 per cent were inclined to disagree, while only 4 per cent were in complete agreement and 8 per cent inclined to agree. 'This statement produced a stronger and more unanimous response than any of the other statements offered to the girls for their reactions.'[9]

The care of the family *is* of great concern to girls and women - and should be to all boys and men and the whole state system - but girls sense, perhaps in the context of the contracting family, labour-saving devices and convenience foods, that they need something more to contribute to personal fulfilment and stability. Writing some years ago in the USA, Irene Peden quoted Dr Bernice Sachs, a specialist in psychosomatic medicine at Seattle University, who was much experienced with women and their problems: 'Many psychiatrists and social workers now feel that a number of women make better mothers and produce healthier children if they do not mother them full-time .... The woman who seeks all the meaning of life in motherhood places on her children a burden their shoulders were never meant to bear - that of providing her with her happiness.'[10] So women *are* working outside the home, contributing to the economy, to the family income and to their own well-being and that of their families. They must be prepared by their education to make the most of employment opportunities.

At present, women are concentrated in a few unskilled, low-paid jobs. Their average hourly earnings in 1981, excluding overtime, were only three-quarters those of men. They are not encouraged to undertake training, forming only 3 per cent of apprentices and 30 per cent of other trainees.[11] Most women are in continuous employment between the ages of 20 and 59, with an average break of only seven years while they care for young children: this negates the view that time and money spent on training women is wasted when they marry and have children.

Some skilled and semi-skilled areas of traditional work for women are contracting: teaching, as school rolls fall, and clerical and secretarial work, as the microprocessor transforms office practice. In the case of the latter, studies have shown that new jobs may be created, but will be more technical in nature.[12]

Given the extent of women's work and its important role in the identity of women, schools are failing girls if they do not encourage them to take a long-term view of their likely employment patterns and equip them to make the most of training opportunities in a changing society. This means that many more girls should continue with the study of mathematics and the physical sciences. But it is not only because the physical sciences are important foundations for employment that we are concerned when girls abandon them so early. When decisions are made not to study a subject at 13+ a barrier is likely to be set up against the image of that rejected subject area: it may be distanced or belittled to justify its rejection. In a study of adolescent girls' understanding of 'forms of knowledge', J.P. Ward reports, 'the girls saw the empirical-technological world (the world of nature and man's exploitation of it) as something huge that frightened them.'[13]

The women students with whom the writer came in contact, during eight years of teaching within science education in a college of education, displayed not so much a dislike of the physical sciences, as an alienation from them. They apologised for their inadequacies. 'I wasn't good enough to do physics,' they would say, and showed a high degree of insecurity when asked to undertake even the simplest investigation that might be carried out in a primary school. It seems that, within physical science, the concern to select and train future scientists has caused secondary schools to ignore the educational needs of the majority of girls. These future teachers in primary schools were in no way prepared to use the exploration of young children into their physical environment as the powerful tool for language and number development that it can be, nor to encourage enquiry-learning skills. The use of the Schools Council's Science 5-13 Project[14] is severely limited by young women's fear of science. If the majority of women experience this sense of alienation from, and fear of, the technological world their contribution as citizens to decison-making in the development and use of products of technology will be immensely impaired. Moreover, to live in fear of one of the major shapers of one's society is surely a serious hazard for mental health.

In conclusion, our concern is that the present pattern of girls' curricular choices away from science disadvantages society by inadequately preparing girls for their roles of worker and decision-maker, and deprives women of much varied, interesting and remunerative employment and, perhaps more seriously, a sense of competence within the society in which they live. The will to change the situation will derive from assumptions about women's roles on the part of those with the power to initiate change. But if effective strategies for change are to be developed, it is important to understand how the situation arises. Reference has already been made to the operation of sex-role stereotyping; in Chapter 3 further research and comment that may give insight to the problem, and its possible solution, will be reviewed.

3. ILLUMINATING THE PROBLEM

Several factors have been put forward to account for differences in achievement between males and females in the physical sciences. Among these are differences in abilities, personality, the image of science, school context, out-of-school experiences, type of science course, teacher characteristics, methods of assessment and the option system, with its associated guidance and counselling. Evidence relating to each of these will be considered in the following sections.

In discussing 'achievement', the focus of attention is sometimes the low representation of girls and women in various activities relating to physical science and it is in this context that concern was expressed in Chapter 2. But achievement is also discussed in terms of their performance when girls do undertake the study of the physical sciences; in this context questions of ability are raised.

There is a growing body of literature relating to girls and science. The DES policy of analysing and publishing the results of public examinations annually makes available useful data. Additionally, as part of the International Study of Educational Attainment (IEA) in 1970, data on science achievement in nineteen countries were collected. The initial analysis of this latter survey drew attention to sex differences in mean scores obtained,[15] but did not control for variable participation in formal science learning. A. Kelly[16] examined and reported on the IEA data in more detail and this provided the framework for a major publication[17] reporting on theoretical positions, research studies and personal perspectives of pupils and teachers, on girls' place in science education. In 1977/78 the science HMIs undertook a study of a limited number of mixed schools in which girls chose in relatively large numbers to study the physical sciences.[18] Science was also an aspect of the secondary survey (*Aspects of Secondary Education in England*)[19] which included a very much larger national sample of schools. These and other sources are used in the following discussions.

The question of ability

The secondary survey reported that some teachers perceived physics as being too difficult for girls,[20] thereby implying that boys and girls are different and that girls lack some ability required to study physics. If teachers assume this, then girls will respond by lowering their expectations of themselves and *perform* less well, whatever their 'ability'.*

In the IEA study, Kelly[22] found that although mean scores varied greatly between the nineteen countries, boys achieved higher scores in all of them than girls did. Differences were smallest in biology and largest in physics and 'practical' (a written test relating to laboratory exercises). The differences in the physical sciences scores were reduced, but by no means removed, however, when girls had studied as much science as the boys had; this was especially true for chemistry. The differences were present at ten years old and accentuated by fourteen.

No serious study has been reported of the skills required for the pursuit of the physical sciences. It is assumed that competence in mathematics is needed,[23] and that some form of 'spatial ability' is involved.[24]

There is evidence that girls are less successful than boys in public examinations in mathematics. GCE O-level figures in 1979 show girls' percentage pass rate to be six percentiles less than that for boys, who had the larger entry. (The corresponding difference in English language was ten percentiles in favour of girls.) These figures tend to support assumptions about girls' greater command of language and boys' superior mathematical skills. Teachers, who are considerably influenced by the success, or failure, of their pupils in public examinations, may feel justified in their assessment of differential abilities in boys and girls. But we must not lose sight of the fact that examinations test performance and not 'abilities'.

Further discussion of the problem of girls' mathematics education may be found in the mathematics pamphlet in this series,[25] but it may be useful to examine here in some detail one school's response to the problem. Stamford School[26] decided to teach half the top band of the first year intake in single-sex groups in mathematics and science, keeping the other two comparable classes mixed as a control. The girls-only class and one of the mixed classes were given the same teacher. In the event, the science results were not fully reported as changes in staffing occurred which could have influenced outcomes. In mathematics, the initial test score averages showed no significant differences for boys and girls in all classes in question. After fifteen months, however, the average test score for the girls-only group was no different from that of the boys in the mixed group, but the girls in the latter were much less successful.

It was not only the girls' test performance that differed in the two groups: teachers reported greater liveliness, involvement in work and improved relationships with the teacher and between girls in the single-sex group. In science it was reported that the girls in the single-sex group were performing well and average test scores were higher than those for the girls in the mixed group.

---

* Terminology is conceptually confused in this area. A.B. Stillman[21] distinguishes between 'ability', 'aptitude' and 'attainment'.

The report is cautious in recommending the strategy for general use and draws attention to other variables which should be taken into account in a more rigorous study, but states: 'One of the major values of this exercise has been the interest it has sparked among teachers now that an improvement in girls' performance has been shown to be feasible. Classroom strategies for dealing with under-achievement are now more readily discussed .... It is more generally recognized that teacher expectation of boys performing better could have an adverse effect on the girls.' One aspect which is, perhaps, not clearly emphasized in the report is that the effect occurred in spite of the two classes being taught by the same teacher (though a different person in each of the years of the experiment). This raises all kinds of questions about *how* the under-achievement of girls occurs in mixed classes.

E. Maccoby and C. Jacklin[27] reviewed a large number of studies in spatial abilities within a wider study of the psychology of sex differences. The pattern of outcomes for spatial ability tests (Table 2) shows a relation to the age of performer. No significant differences appear in the reported studies before the age of twelve years. Thereafter the male usually obtains a higher mean score, but some studies show that differences tend to disappear with practice.

Table 2 Sex differences in reported research into visual-spatial ability

Visual-spatial ability tests	Age of subjects	No. of studies reported	No. sex difference	Girls' higher mean score	Boys' higher mean score
Non-analytic	up to 14	25	22	2	1
	14+	10	2	0	8
Analytic	up to 14	28	21	4	3
	14+	36	17	0	19

Data extracted from E. Maccoby and C. Jacklin. *The Psychology of Sex Differences* (Wiley, 1975).

The GIST project* discovered an improved performance in a spatial test on the part of girls and boys who had followed a workshop-based course for six months. No such improvement was found for a parallel, mixed group studying home economics.[28] It is difficult to maintain an argument based on innate differences in the face of this evidence.

---

* Girls into Science and Technology project, supported by the Social Science Research Council/EOC Joint Panel on Women and Under-Achievement, the Department of Industry and the Schools Council. GIST Project, Manchester Polytechnic, 9A Didsbury Park, Manchester M20 0LH.

At a conference at Churchill College, Cambridge, Carol Dweck (from the USA) suggested that teachers may be responsible for girls' tendency to underestimate themselves.[29] Her research has observed and coded criticism (negative feedback) given to 9 to 10-year-olds in the classroom. Boys received far more criticism than girls and it was more diffuse. But when it was *work-directed*, almost half was related to non-intellectual performance, whereas only just over 10 per cent of criticism of girls was in non-intellectual aspects of work and nearly 90 per cent of the rest reflected on their ability. The result of this may be that boys and girls come to attribute failure to different sources: the girl to her ability and the boy to lack of effort or to the teacher's 'down' on him. This has implications for resilience in the face of failure. The boy will see a new task or a change of teacher as a fresh opportunity in which, if he cares to make the effort, he will succeed; he will display confidence in his own competence. The girl, on the other hand, may doubt her ability and retreat from the task, showing 'helplessness'.

It was argued that different subjects may require different learning approaches. Language-based disciplines are incremental, building on what has been learnt before, but mathematics and science continually involve new concepts: confusion is more likely to arise in initial stages with each new concept, and a sense of failure is experienced. In such a situation children with a sense of competence will meet the challenge, whereas the 'helpless' children will retreat and assume they are no good at the subject.

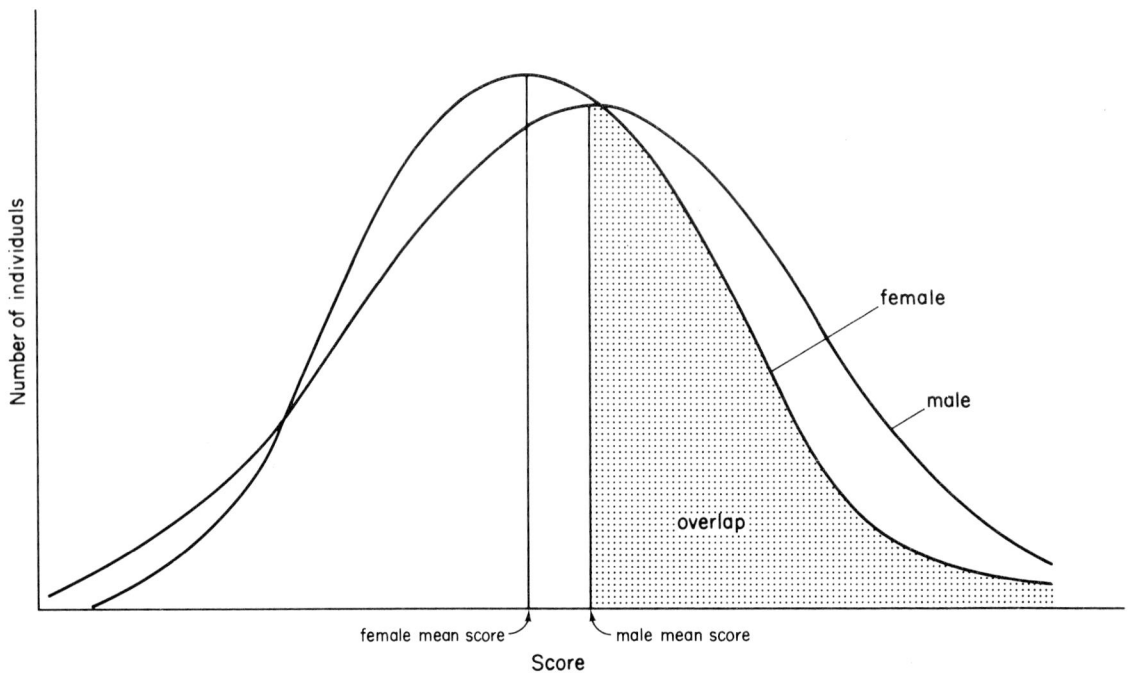

Figure 5   Distribution of typical scores in a test in which males achieve a higher score than females

Much of the evidence for sex differences derives from mean values of scores for males and females, but in focusing on the difference between the groups, the variation within each group is ignored. In general there is a far greater range of ability, whichever characteristic is studied, within any one sex than there is between the sexes. Figure 5 demonstrates this. Each sex shows a normal distribution of the trait under examination. In the typical case given, the mean for the male is greater than the mean for the female, but overlap is considerable. The shaded area indicates the number of women who obtain higher scores than half the men.

J.S. Hyde[30] has reworked the data available in studies reviewed by Maccoby and Jacklin and shows that sex accounted for only approximately 4 per cent of the variance in the spatial ability studies.

Stanley King[31] gives data from tests of 'considerable numbers of school-leavers' (Table 3), emphasizing the 'overlap' between the performance of boys and girls. He stresses that it is in the areas which are most strongly sex-stereotyped in society that the least overlap occurs and concludes that stereotyping gives rise to differences in performance.

Table 3 Sex differences in tests on school-leavers

Skill tested	Sex with better mean	'Overlap'	
Vocabulary	girl	45-50%	Percentage of boys doing better than half the girls
Arithmetic	girl	40-45%	
Reasoning (verbal/number)	girl	40-45%	
Clerical	girl	35-40%	
Mathematics	boy	45%	Percentage of girls doing better than half the boys
Spatial	boy	35-40%	
Mechanical	boy	20-25%	

Source: J.S. King 'Sex differences and careers guidance', *Careers Bulletin*, Department of Employment Careers Services Branch, spring 1976.

There is a growing consensus among psychologists working in the field of sex differences[32] that the detectable differences in abilities between the sexes is very small compared to the large range of abilities displayed within each sex, and can in no way be held responsible for the large differences in 'achievement' of the two sexes in various fields of endeavour. So we must look elsewhere than to abilities for explanations of the major differences in girls' and boys' participation in science.

It is disquieting to learn, in this connection, of the National Foundation for Educational Research's (NFER) battery of tests 'designed to assess individual third and fourth year secondary pupils in five different abilities: symbolic reasoning, mechanical ability, spatial ability, clerical speed and accuracy and scientific reasoning and process'.[33] It is envisaged that schools will use these tests to identify pupils' 'strengths and weaknesses' for future setting. The author, A. Stillman, is careful to point out that 'an ability score represents no more than a measure of one person's strength in that ability at that time - it is still not a measure of things to come. If, however, the test is used with a large number of students and their progress is monitored over a period of years, then it may be possible to give the test a measure of predictability. This test would then be known to measure this student's aptitude in this area.'

We are back in the era of IQ sorting. Has Mr Stillman never heard of the self-fulfilling prophecy?

The question of personality

Research studies that have aimed at relating personality characteristics to the pursuit of science have been reviewed by J. Head.[34] The physical scientist emerges, typically, as an emotionally reticent male who is imbued with the Protestant ethic valuing hard work, more interested in things than in people, more authoritarian and conservative than those in comparative groups and whose preferred mode of thinking is convergent.

Such a person will be attracted to a science presented as objective, unemotional and governed by immutable laws. He will tend, therefore, to perpetuate these images of science and the scientist. If women and girls are more interested in people and in relationships than in things and are encouraged to be emotionally expressive, then this presentation of science will not appeal to them.

Head has carried out work himself[35] in connection with the Concepts in Secondary Mathematics and Science Project at Chelsea College, and has explored further the relationship between personality and science choice. He found that, even at fourteen years, the boys who chose science were more authoritarian than the girls or the other boys, and that they possessed fewer doubts or uncertainties. They gave cut-and-dried answers in completion of sentence stems, whereas other boys and most girls showed an awareness of alternative ways of behaving in indicated relationships or situations. The girls choosing science, though few in number, seemed to be among the most mature in his sample.[36] They differed from other girls in that they displayed a somewhat lower self-esteem, a characteristic also detected by A. Smithers and J. Collings[37] in girls studying science in the sixth form. This last study also found that the girl physical scientists were less 'person-orientated' than other girls.

Such evidence has led Head[38] to relate science choice to Marcia's model of personality development, in which the major task facing the adolescent is the gaining of a mature 'ego-identity'. There are several ways in which the young person may move towards this goal, Marcia argues, and two processes are involved: 'crisis' (a questioning of beliefs or values) and 'commitment' (the embracing of certain beliefs about oneself and the world).

(a) Crisis and commitment may occur together gradually, in which case adolescent development may be relatively trouble-free.

(b) A period of acute doubting and questioning may occur (known as 'moratorium') before personal beliefs are sorted out: this represents the popular view of the rebellious unreliable teenager.

(c) Young people may not question the beliefs and values of their immediate circle until some crisis occurs, such as leaving home, which may result in severe problems (for example, 'dropping out') before a mature ego-identity is achieved.

(d) Adolescent beliefs may be clung to determinedly without any questioning at all (known as 'foreclosure').

Head's suggestion is that if these models are valid, the question of science choice may be affected as follows:

> boys at the foreclosure stage may choose science without much thought, as they are expected to, but may later question this choice (the 'swing from science' at A level and university)
>
> boys who continue with science may be those who are delaying their own questioning indefinitely: these are those who perpetuate the conventional view of the scientist
>
> girls at the foreclosure stage may reject science unless strong pressure is put on them
>
> girls at the moratorium stage may choose science defiantly or with greater maturity after assessing its value to society.

However, the kind of science presented in physics and chemistry in the third year - abstract, difficult and rarely showing relevance to social issues[39] - is unlikely to attract questioning adolescents of either sex.

Only a small proportion of pupils will have achieved a mature ego by the age of thirteen or fourteen years, when they are asked to make subject choices. Head argues that 'most girls entering science are probably at this stage as they will need some self-examination and sense of commitment to make this unconventional choice'.

The value of a model such as the one above, posited by Head, is that personality development can be linked with subject choice and thus it is possible to make predictions about the outcomes of possible changes in the curriculum. Head discusses three alternatives: (i) *delaying subject choice*, which might lead to fewer boys choosing science, whilst those boys and girls who so choose will be more mature and possibly have more flexible minds; (ii) *giving science a more feminine image* by making girls more visible in textbooks, etc. which might increase recruitment of girls at the foreclosure stage but, unless the change was massive, this would leave boys unaffected, and (iii) *emphasizing the applications and relevance of science* to the issues that concern the thinking adolescent. Head argues that this last alternative is the only one that will attract more girls and boys at the moratorium stage, and will also produce a more imaginative, flexible scientist with a less stereotyped masculine image.

It may be necessary to use all three strategies. Certainly the position of the sciences in the option system is problematical at present, and is discussed in more detail later. A possible resolution of imbalance in the curriculum, or within science, would be the inclusion of a broad-based science course in the 'core' of the curriculum for both girls and boys.

The masculine image of science does less than justice to the many women already working in science and technology. To counteract this, several initiatives have been launched. The Industry/Education Unit of the Department of Industry has sponsored a film showing young women engineers.[40] The EOC are producing a series of posters showing women in science.[41] The Careers Research and Advisory Centre has published a paperback book containing 'personal stories and advice from 84 women in industry and commerce', and General Electric Company have produced a booklet, *Women in Research in GEC*, describing women working in their several research departments.[42]

G. Walford[43] has shown the extent of the bias to the male in language, reference and illustration in physics textbooks and recommends that all future texts attempt to represent males and females equally.

Finally, science should not be presented only as a system of abstract concepts and immutable laws applicable to laboratory situations, but as a human endeavour with philosophical, economic, social and cultural implications.

The question of school context

A classic study of the effects of school context on educational outcomes for boys and girls is R.R. Dale's comparison of co-educational and single-sex schools.[44] Although this work was largely carried out before 1951* it is still quoted extensively. His surveys revealed greater social and personal benefits accruing from the mixed schools in terms of remembered enjoyment of school and of relationships with teachers and with peers of the opposite sex. He also demonstrated, from examination data, that boys achieve better academic results in mixed schools than in boys' schools. The results for girls were less clear - in science they were more successful in girls' schools. But he found that the girls from mixed schools were younger, drawn from city rather than rural areas and were entered for more subjects than were those from girls' schools. He argued that these factors disadvantaged the co-educated girls and so assumed that the effect was as for boys: an academic advantage in co-education.

---

* Some more recent data from Northern Ireland were included, but here mixed and single sex schools are often state and church, Protestant and Catholic, respectively. These very different contexts make generalizations from the data of doubtful validity.

Table 4

Numbers of subjects in which girls or boys from single-sex or mixed schools obtained the highest percentage of passes, and the highest percentage of grades 'A' in O-level examinations, by type of school (London Board, 1973)

Number of highest percentages

	in overall passes		*in grades A*	
Type of group	Grammar	Comprehensive	Grammar	Comprehensive
Girls in girls' schools	7 (1=)	4 (3=)	5	3 (2=)
Girls in mixed schools	4 (1=)	2	3	2 (1=)
Boys in mixed schools	1	3 (2=)	2	2
Boys in boys' schools	0	1 (1=)	3	4

Numbers of subjects in which girls or boys from single-sex or mixed schools obtained the lowest percentage of passes, and the lowest percentage of grades 'A' in O-level examinations, by type of school (London Board, 1973)

Number of lowest percentages

	in overall passes		*in grades A*	
Type of group	Grammar	Comprehensive	Grammar	Comprehensive
Girls in girls' schools	0	2 (1=)	0 (1=)	2
Girls in mixed schools	3	4 (1=)	4 (1=)	4
Boys in mixed schools	4 (2=)	1 (1=)	6 (1=)	2
Boys in boys' schools	4 (2=)	4 (1=)	1 (1=)	5

The study included a total of 13 subjects.
The figures in brackets indicate additional positions shared with other groups.
The arrows show the direction of organizational trends from single sex grammar schools to mixed comprehensives.

Source: R. Wood and C. Ferguson. 'Unproven case for coeducation', *Times Educational Supplement*, 4 October 1974.

Following the publication of Dale's book in 1974, R. Wood and C. Ferguson[45] examined more contemporary data from some 100,000 pupils entering for London O-level examinations in 1973. They found, for grammar schools, that Dale's case for superior performance of boys in mixed schools was unproven but 'the girls from girls-only schools have the edge in the majority of subjects'. They drew attention to the high percentage passes in physics and chemistry from girls' schools and to the 'dramatically high pass rate' of co-educated girls in Nuffield Chemistry. When the data for comprehensive schools were examined, the London board data showed less school-dependent variation and Wood and Ferguson saw this to be 'an encouraging sign if the mixed comprehensive school is to be the school of the future'. However, if one examines the change in relative success of groups of girls and boys across the organizational change from single-sex grammar to mixed comprehensive, a disturbing situation emerges, as Table 4 shows. In all four comparisons the success of girls is reduced and in percentage passes the boys improve (although not in percentage A grades). This may result from improved performance by boys but we must be cautious lest an equalizing effect arises from the girls lowering their expectations.

Further evidence of the influence of context on performance of girls was obtained from research carried out by the author in 1975 with the help of Jan Craig. This has been reported elsewhere.[46] We set out to examine girls' and boys' performance in Nuffield and more conventional examinations, but controlled for type of school in sampling. Analyses showed no overall differences in percentage passes for girls and boys, whichever type of course was examined, but when sub-groups from different types of school were compared, it was found that a greater range of percentage pass figures were obtained for the girls than for the boys. The performance of the latter was relatively independent of type of school in terms of mixed or co-educational. Table 5 sets out figures for the conventional physics examination, showing the superior performance of girls in girls' schools. Not every examination showed such a clear-cut pattern, but similar trends were apparent in the other five sets of data.

Table 5 Percentage passes for subsamples of boys and girls in the 'conventional' physics examination

School type	Boys	Girls
	%	%
Single sex:		
Direct grant and independent	62.3	78.6
Grammar	67.9	75.5
Comprehensive	50.5	57.1
Mixed:		
Grammar	72.0	60.0
Comprehensive	59.3	46.0

Source: J. Harding and J. Craig. 'Girls and science education report'. 1978. Available from Chelsea College, CSME Library, Bridges Place, London SW6 4HR.

The variability in the involvement of girls in physical science from one school to another was visible in statistics collected by the author from local education authorities in 1975. The author has argued elsewhere[47] that it is not the type of school *per se* that creates a difference but the expectation of girls found in the school, whether it be mixed or for girls only. Girls' grammar schools, many of them descendants of the early girls' schools set up a century ago with the avowed aim to give girls an education equal to that of their brothers, were more likely to convey high expectations of achievement to their pupils than were comprehensive schools containing a high proportion of girls for whom the educational objectives had been publicly stated to be the production of good wives and mothers.[48] A large number of comprehensive schools have grown from secondary modern schools by expansion. The expectation of girls in these may account for the low success of girls in comprehensive schools in the Wood and Ferguson figures.

A suggestion was made in 1975 that mixed comprehensive schools which were unusually successful in attracting girls into the physical sciences should be studied carefully to identify the constellation of factors associated with this success. It was for this purpose that data mentioned above were obtained from LEAs. In the event, research funding was not forthcoming but the Inspectorate carried out their own survey which has recently been published.[49]

Other factors in the school context may affect girls and boys differently. For example, there are large differences in the way schools present options in the choice of subjects. (This is discussed below, under 'The question of subject choice, guidance and counselling'.) The availability of resources is another variant. Where facilities are in short supply, girls may lose out. The HMI, reporting on the secondary survey,[50] state that, at the time of writing, up to 20 per cent more science teachers would be needed to provide science for all, equivalent to one-sixth of the curriculum. In addition, 40 per cent more laboratory accommodation would be required. 'Evidence ... suggests that boys may be given preference, particularly in physics, if numbers have to be limited because of shortage of staff or accommodation.'[51] This demonstrates a school's assumption that physics is less important for girls. E. Byrne[52] presents evidence that the less able girl in a rural school has a triple chance of deprivation, as resources are likely to be allocated to more able rather than to less able, to boys rather than to girls and to urban rather than to rural schools. She strongly challenges the assumptions behind these differentials.

The question of out-of-school experiences
───

Attention has been drawn by many authors[53] to the different early experiences of boys and girls. Boys are stimulated physically from a very early age[54] but girls are pacified. The toys each sex is given differ greatly. Girls are more likely to receive dolls, a pram, a doll's house and miniature kitchen equipment, while boys get toy cars, construction kits, working models, miniature tools, guns, chemistry sets and computer games. One astute manufacturer has extended the doll market to boys by launching 'Action-man'. E. Byrne[55] has described how manufacturers label the appropriate sex for a toy or game by the illustrations carried on the packaging. The outcome is that each sex learns appropriate roles, including acceptable emotions (girls –

caring; boys - aggression) but also different kinds of manipulation, in that girls' toys rarely take apart nor are they designed to interact with other materials and seldom do they use electrical sources or equipment such as bulbs and transformers. The early experiences of boys therefore give a much more appropriate foundation for the physical sciences than do those of girls.

An American study reported by P. Torrance[56] illustrates how powerfully these experiences may constrain the performance of girls in science. He was investigating measures of 'creativity' with children aged eight to eleven by asking them to suggest a variety of uses for science-based toys such as magnets, lenses and springs and to explain how they worked. The girls refused at first to participate, objecting that 'these are boys' toys'. When persuaded to take part, they performed much less well than the boys did, in the judgement of adult observers. Torrance was shocked by the inhibiting effect of this stereotyping of activities, and talked with parents (who were mostly colleagues on the university staff) and with teachers of the campus school which the children attended. The following year, when he tested a comparable group of children, the girls readily took part and scored as high as the boys did. This study gives encouragement to those wanting to change girls' participation in the more technical sciences, as it shows their expectation of themselves may be readily changed, given appropriate encouragement from significant adults.

Another study in the USA[57] shows that out-of-school activities of older students may continue to vary and may have implications for science teaching. High school students following the Harvard Project Physics course were asked to report the amount of time they spent on about 60 different science-related activities. These reports were computer analysed and generated five factors. Two of these, labelled 'academic' and 'cosmology' showed no significant difference between girls and boys, while two others, 'nature study' and 'applications to life', occupied the girls rather more than the boys. But a fifth factor, representing more than one-third of all the variance in the sample, was 'tinkering' - the girls just didn't spend time taking their motor bikes to bits! Again, the girls would be disadvantaged for laboratory-based investigations by this difference in experience, although the 'applications to life' emphasis gives a lead to their interests that should be exploited.

The author has noticed that a very recent development in this country - 'space invaders' - is attracting young (and older) boys, but not girls. This is likely to create a friendly association with computers on the part of the former that the latter will not experience. It will be sad if the new technology also becomes stereotyped as a male preserve, and there are indications that this may be happening.

The question of the kind of science course

Science offered to children in the eleven to sixteen curriculum usually takes the form of integrated or combined courses in the first two years, followed by the separate sciences in year three, which is also almost invariably the year when option choices are made for examination courses in the separate sciences in years four and five. Year three may therefore be the terminal course in more than one science for many of the pupils.* In the mixed schools selected by HMI for their survey because of the relatively high involvement of girls in the physical sciences, the teachers were aware of this. They also saw year three as a time when pupils got 'a taste' of individual sciences to inform their choices, but many taught as if year three was the 'launch pad' for the later years and so focused attention on those who would continue to study their subject, particularly in physics and chemistry. As a consequence, whereas years one and two were frequently geared to the interests of the pupils and contained a great many practical investigations, the work in year three became more abstract, the pace accelerated and practical work gave way, to a large extent, to more passive learning such as note-taking, even in those schools.[59]

How did girls appear to respond to this situation? Some teachers have commented to the author[60] that 'girls don't like practical work', 'girls prefer to make neat drawings and take notes', and 'girls can't handle the enquiry method'. The Inspectors, on the other hand, reported that although girls were more tentative in their approach to laboratory work, 'One of the most prominent factors detected in the enquiry was the high value girls placed on practical work.... Even among those girls who had dropped science it was remarkable how many commented favourably on their attitude to the laboratory work of earlier years.'[61] Nor was there evidence that they were opposed to a problem-solving approach - in fact, many expressed the view that they preferred to be involved in their own experimental work and 'to sort out their own ideas'.

Although girls showed more care in the presentation of drawings and written work, which the Inspectors attributed to their earlier maturation, 'girls did not wish to encourage an emphasis on passive note-taking'. One girl is quoted as saying: 'Because we are good at written work I wish that teachers would not assume that we actually like this method of working or that we learn much by it.' From this it seems that some teachers have quite the wrong idea about what motivates girls in science lessons!

Alison Kelly[62] reports some interesting responses by teachers to her query as to why girls fail to do better in science. One letter in particular seems very perceptive of girls' approaches to their learning. A male head of physics attempts to ascertain what he calls the 'class personality' - its preferred ways of working and interests. When introducing a topic he initiates a 'literature search' linking syllabus topics to girls' interests, makes use of their liking for coloured drawings by including much information on annotated drawings and diagrams and provides security in experimental work by ensuring that they know exactly what is required of them. He goes on to claim, 'Once they have done it right and written it right they are then relaxed. They like to get their duty done. Once they have done their duty they return to the experiment and start playing with it, exploring new effects, discovering, asking endless questions. So what I have

---

* Only 42 per cent of boys and 24 per cent of girls continue to study more than one science subject in year four, although a small portion of the rest (more boys than girls) may continue with a single subject integrated science course.[58]

learnt is that they progress according to the motto: 'duty before discovery'. Possibly boys like it the other way round.'[63] The greater conformity of girls, whatever its origin, has been accepted by this teacher who is prepared to work through it and enable them to go beyond it.

D. Ebbutt investigated the tendency of girls and boys in the mixed junior science classes he taught to label topics either as 'boys' science' or 'girls' science'. He suggests that the criterion used to label a piece of science as girls' was that it should have some tangible end product (extracting plant scents, making crystals, 'tie dye' from plant extracts, felt pen chromatograms). He suggests these 'are nearer to a craft-type activity than the more usual understanding or controlling type of science'. In the absence of a product, Ebbutt suggests that some girls will substitute a neat book with painstakingly drawn and labelled diagrams 'at the same time demonstrating a depressingly low level of involvement in practical work, or a similarly low level of concept development, or both'.[64]

Ebbutt may be right in stressing the importance of the *product*, but this may be yet another example of girls needing to recognize that an activity has some purpose, that it is relevant for them. What Ebbutt describes may be the younger girls' response to this need.

The relevance of science to their lives seemed to be a particular need for girls in the HMI enquiry.[65] M.B. Ormerod[66] has also linked a concern for the social implications of science and a liking for the subject, in the case of thirteen-year-old girls. He recommended some time ago[67] that these aspects should be introduced into science courses for the years eleven to fourteen, before choices were made. An emphasis on the relevance of physical science to the problems identified by thinking adolescents is also recommended by Head, as argued in an earlier section, to increase the number of girls choosing the physical sciences and the quality of both girls and boys so choosing.[68] The Inspectors comment that the problems associated with examination orientation in science is especially detrimental to girls.

A very few schools in England do not offer separate science subjects in the option system, but expect all pupils to continue the study of science up to the age of sixteen, either as integrated science (usually as the equivalent of two examination subjects) or as biological science and physical science. Three of the total of 21 schools visited by the Inspectors in their enquiry operated one of these systems (a higher proportion than in the country as a whole). In none of the three was there marked resentment over the compulsion to continue with all the sciences; indeed, several girls are quoted as favouring the system,[69] but in these schools the broader courses had enabled the teachers 'to take account of the wider range of interests of their pupils, both boys and girls'.

The question of teacher characteristics

Girls and boys appear to prefer different styles of teaching. A report by J. Eggleston *et al*[70] found that teaching styles are remarkably stable, although some teachers did modify their style to suit different groups of pupils. Their observations in O-level science classes identified three styles: Style I, 'The problem solvers' where initiative was held by the teachers who, by questioning, challenged the pupils to observe, speculate and solve problems; Style II, 'The informers' who presented a 'non-practical, fact-acquiring image' and Style III, 'The enquirers' who used pupil-centred enquiry methods. Style I was popular with boys but not so with girls, while Style III was most effective for girls in maintaining a liking for physics and chemistry. More women teachers than men used Style III. Nearly half the men used Style I; the greater expectation of men to command may be apparent here. M. Galton[71] suggests that girls may dislike the 'direct-questioning, problem-solving' approach which they may meet most frequently in mixed physical sciences classes with men teachers. That this may be so is supported by girls' comments included in the 'personal experience' section of Kelly's book.[72] Many of these indicate girls' embarrassment when, as a minority group in a predominantly male class, they are asked to respond publicly. On the other hand, their resentment in being ignored is also indicated. The Inspectors, too, detected these responses in girls.[73] It seems that Style III - removing public interaction with the teacher - may enable girls to participate more fully in the class activity, sorting things out for themselves.

Girls' comments[74] give evidence of their intense dislike of rowdy behaviour among boys in science classes, which sometimes includes overt sexist comments about girls or women. If this is not controlled by the teachers or, worse, if they are seen to condone it, great resentment is aroused in the girls. That they can come to terms with this and fight back to self-respect is illustrated by Mani and Donna, lone girls in a fourth-year physics class with a male teacher.[75] These girls were helped by a female teacher in the school, who stepped in initially to help with their problems in physics, but through discussion enabled them to understand what was going on socially in the classroom and to take a positive approach which changed their own behaviour and that of the boys.

Male teachers were not always reported as unhelpful, however. Girls commented on their good teaching and on their kindness and patience in explaining things without making them feel foolish.[76]

It has been suggested that the sex of the teacher may influence girls' choice of science by the presence or absence of role models for them to follow.[77] Certainly, as part of their perception of the maleness of the physical sciences, girls commented that few of the teachers of these subjects were women.[78] On the other hand, girls also perceive that a woman teacher can have a 'down' on girls and favour the boys in the class.[79] However, it seems from the evidence of teacher influence on girls' choice of science and their enjoyment of it that teaching style and individual behaviour may be more influential than the sex of the teacher.

The question of assessment

The science HMIs are increasingly making known their belief that the examinations in science that face young people at 16+ are exerting undue pressure on the science curriculum.[80] They claim that 'Opinions expressed by teachers and pupils suggest that examinations at present make unrealistic demands, and radical changes may be required if teachers are further to develop teaching methods designed to encourage more girls to take physics and chemistry.[81]

Ormerod and Duckworth[82] summarized research studies on comparative standards of examination subjects. The Joint Matriculation Board (JMB) and the Welsh Board had each carried out such studies on O-level results in the early 1970s. In every case, physics and chemistry (followed by French) emerged as the most difficult subjects. An NFER enquiry, covering the results from four examination boards and using four methods for comparing relative subject difficulty reported that, at GCE O level, chemistry and physics are the two most severely graded subjects; physics was less severely graded in the CSE. It seems therefore that the girls and the Inspectors make justifiable criticisms.

A further factor to be considered is the type of assessment used. The last fifteen years of examining have seen the introduction of new methods of assessment. Machine-marked, multiple-choice items appeared initially in physical science papers but are increasingly being used for public examinations in other subjects. The advent of the microprocessor has extended their use to school examinations.

There are now several studies that show that boys are more successful than girls in answering multiple-choice items. The author investigated the performance of boys and girls in six O-level science examinations in 1974.[83] Briefly, the findings were that in three of the four multiple-choice papers boys did significantly better than girls, although there were no differences in overall percentage passes in any of the examinations. In the one essay-type paper included in the study, girls were more successful than boys. Papers carrying structured questions were answered equally well by both sexes.

C. Ferguson[84] has shown that when the London University Schools Examination Board introduced a multiple-choice paper into the O-level biology examination, a clear differentiation was obtained. The same group of boys did better than the girls in the multiple-choice paper and less well than the girls in the longer answer papers. This was repeated the following year.

More recently, R.J.L. Murphy[85] has demonstrated that, in a range of subjects examined by the AEB with a multiple-choice paper as well as another using a different assessment technique, the boys improved their performance relative to the girls when the multiple-choice papers were compared to the others.

This presents a dilemma for examiners which many do not, as yet, recognize. It is assumed that the method of assessment is unbiased, although suspicion has fallen on the 'subjectivity' of essay marking. For many, the multiple-choice paper is an *objective* test*, removing this subjectivity. The tendency is to assume that we have been

---

* There appears to be a conceptual confusion in the use of this term. Some teachers use it as above in its adjectival form, others use it as a noun and claim that the multiple-choice format tests *objectives* more effectively than do other forms of assessment.

penalizing boys (with poorer verbal skills) for years and now have a
'pure' mode of assessment in the multiple-choice format (as well as one
that gives extensive syllabus coverage and is more conveniently marked).
However, we know little about the skills that are required to achieve
well in a multiple-choice test and we may be neglecting to nurture
communication and reflective skills that other techniques of assessment
encourage, if we abandon them. As the author has argued elsewhere,[86]
we must ask how validly the assessment matches the understanding
possessed by the candidate and how well the skills we are assessing
match the skills that are required in future practice within the subject
area. A report published by the National Assessment of Educational
Progress in the USA is critical of the extended use of multiple-choice
testing there.[87] Students are able to 'formulate quick and short
formulations' but seem 'genuinely puzzled' at requests to explain or
defend their points of view.

Two sub-groups within the author's study did not fit the common
pattern of girls doing less well in multiple-choice papers: girls in
mixed schools following Nuffield Chemistry and those following Nuffield
Physics courses. They were from a smaller number of schools than other
sub-samples but one can ask what it was about those girls - the schools,
the teachers, or the course they were following - which made them
atypical. More research is needed in this area.

It is on record that the National Assessment of Educational Progress[88]
has identified a lower achievement in females across the areas of science,
mathematics and social sciences using machine-marked tests. The IEA
tests referred to earlier (p.17) were all multiple-choice items and
this may have contributed to the overall better performance of the male.

It is unfortunate that the greater use of multiple-choice papers in
school science examinations will undoubtedly convey to girls a greater
sense of their own inadequacies.

The question of subject choice, guidance and counselling

Most secondary schools offer a 'core' of compulsory subjects, supple-
mented by optional subjects, to pupils in the fourth and fifth forms.
The provision of choice at this stage is believed to increase pupils'
motivation and enable them to respond with an increasing awareness of
their own strengths and weaknesses. But the author has argued elsewhere[89] that the power sustaining sex differentiation in science
education arises from socially derived stereotypes of male and female
behaviour and the option system, together with the position of science
subjects within it, is one of the controls through which it operates.

The organization of core and options varies from school to school,
but some general picture of comprehensive schools may be gathered from
the sample of 92 such schools in the secondary survey. In most, the
core was allocated less than 50 per cent of curricular time and
consisted of English language, mathematics and perhaps two other subjects
in which physical education, religious education and careers education
appeared most frequently. Science was part of the core in only 11 per
cent of schools; in others it was included in the options. In 90 per
cent of the schools, these consisted of 17-28 subjects arranged in
'blocks' usually five or six in number.[90]

Within this system, girls and boys are required to make decisions that may have an irrevocable effect on future opportunities. The choice away from the physical sciences comes into this category, as it is very difficult to take them up again at a later stage.

At the present time physics, chemistry and biology are in competition with each other (and, to a lesser extent, with some form of combined science) in the option system. The problem is that if pupils choose all three sciences, their curriculum is likely to lack balance, being biased to science at the expense of the creative subjects, while choice between the sciences leads to a distorted and biased science education. Most schools, however, require pupils to choose at least one science subject. The outcome is the sex-differentiated pattern outlined in Chapter 2 and the problem facing those who want to involve more girls in the physical sciences is how to persuade them to choose these when their interests may lie in other directions.

The most important criterion for a choice of subject in the eyes of pupils and their parents* is that it should be useful to a future career.[91] Many girls are not ready to commit themselves to a particular career at the age of fourteen and so a sensitive and responsible guidance and counselling system is needed to ensure that no career door is closed by a pre-emptive choice.

Evidence from a small survey quoted by Kelly[92] suggests that boys may be overestimating the usefulness of science to their anticipated careers (for example, in accountancy, banking and law), whereas girls are underestimating the value of the physical sciences to careers such as nursing and catering. Either these girls are unaware of the contribution of a particular science to the work they have in mind, or else science is so far from their self-image that they cannot contemplate it.

Ebbutt[93] attempted to assess grammar school girls' image of a woman scientist. She emerged as 'sensible, capable, reliable, cool, calm, logical, positive, orderly, exact, technical and dedicated', attributes which Ebbutt speculates are diametrically opposite to those forming the self-image of most third-year girls.

Too often the subject background of the teacher in a position to advise is found to correlate with decisions made for and against science,[94] indicating that, intentionally or not, the interests of teachers may be influencing those they are advising.

The Girls and Physical Science sub-committee of the Association for Science Education has been collecting *ad hoc* strategies teachers have been using to improve girls' involvement in the physical sciences. Three which have been remarkably successful have been published in the Association's bulletin.

---

* The Equal Opportunities Commission has prepared a free leaflet advising parents on option choices: 'Getting it right matters' (1982). Education Section, EOC, Overseas House, Quay Street, Manchester M3 3HN.

In one case, all the teachers in the science department were determined to change the existing low numbers of girls in physics and chemistry.[95] They discussed career choices carefully with the girls, encouraged them to recognize their own ability, presented the case for keeping options open to parents and arranged for girls to be seen demonstrating physical science and technological apparatus on open days. The head of science, a keen photographer, photographed girls involved in this kind of work and pinned enlarged reproductions of the prints on corridor walls so that the girls could see themselves being scientists.

A second strategy was applied in a girls' school which was about to become amalgamated with a boys' school.[96] In the previous year, no girls had chosen physics in the fourth year. The careers teacher (an historian) was concerned. She had developed a tape/slide sequence at a previous school, informing girls of the careers open to them if they kept on with the study of physics. With the co-operation of a temporary head of science (a woman biologist who regretted her own lack of physics), this tape/slide presentation was shown by the latter in each third-year science class towards the end of the autumn term. This was accompanied by information saying that they had to choose at least one science subject from a list of eight. They were asked to take a simple form home to discuss the matter with their parents and return the form with their possible choice marked on it. No name was required on the form, so that the girls should not feel they were having to make a decision before the official option choices were to be made in the spring term. The reason for this procedure was ostensibly to inform the head of science of the possible demand from which to group the options, but in the event it caused the girls to think seriously about science before competing demands of other subjects were apparent. It was this strategy, as well as the information about careers, to which the teachers attributed the outcome of 52 girls in the year group choosing physics. In the mixed school, girls and boys were almost equally represented in the resulting classes.

The third example was from a school which participated in the 16+ trials in physics.[97] The head of science claims that as no ability bar operates in moving from third to fourth year, both girls and boys continue to study the subject in large numbers.

It is apparent that availability of information about careers, the restricting self-image of girls and the expectations of all who are in a position to influence them are important factors which should be considered in developing sensitive and responsible counselling services.

4. WHAT ACTION CAN WE TAKE?

In order to improve the achievement of girls in science, by increasing the number continuing with the study of the physical sciences after the age of fourteen, and enabling them to do this with enjoyment and success, initiatives must be taken at various levels: national, local and in the schools. Some of the changes recommended below will not take place until consensus is achieved nationally, but it is possible for every single teacher in the school system to make some change which may help individual girls to take advantage of the opportunities offered in education or employment. This may be in the way they present the teaching/learning experience to girls, in the expectations they hold for girls and boys or in the way they relate to them. Even teachers in boys' schools are influential, through the ways they encourage boys to think about women and about their relationships with them, for girls' science education is shaped by the view society has of women.

These recommendations are made in terms of the following assumptions:

(1) the place of science and technology in our society is such that all young people should continue with their education in these areas to the end of compulsory schooling;

(2) the pursuit of one specialist science subject does not fulfil the requirement in (1);

(3) the overlap in measured abilities between girls and boys is large and the differences in no way justify the curricular differences now existing;

(4) stereotyping by sex disadvantages both men and women in our society.

Action at the teacher level

Teachers are important because they mediate between pupils and the subjects they study. Their expectations are conveyed to boys and girls in many explicit and subtle ways. On them depends the structure for learning in the classroom or laboratory; they choose and present curricular materials and activities. They endorse or correct their pupils' behaviour and thereby reinforce or challenge established attitudes and assumptions.

Recognition of the problem

If teachers are to involve girls more actively in physical science topics and enable them to choose physics and chemistry when choice is offered in the curriculum, the most important prerequisite is for them to recognize that the present low involvement of girls in these subjects is a problem (for the girls and for society more generally) and actively want to do something about it. Once this is accepted, there are many ways of tackling the problem.

Recognition of disadvantage

Teachers should be aware that girls come to lessons in physics and chemistry doubly disadvantaged: in earlier experiences and in their own self-image in relation to science. They are likely to have had less experience of constructional, electrical and mechanical toys and of chemistry sets than boys have had. In addition, 'scientists' of all kinds are usually presented as male. Girls will therefore feel less confident when faced with science equipment, see themselves as less able than boys in science and even feel that it is inappropriate for them to be involved. This is especially true in the physical sciences. The biological sciences provide links for girls in subject matter which relates to food and to their own bodies; moreover, there is a strong expectation in schools that girls should study biology.

Equality of expectation

But, while recognizing these disadvantages, teachers should never show surprise at lack of experience or comment on lack of confidence that girls may exhibit. They should present work as if they expected no difference in involvement or achievement between boys and girls.

Paradoxically, this may require different approaches for the two sexes as boys, typically, need challenging to think through what they are required to do before plunging into the activities, while girls may hesitate, occupy themselves with writing or drawing, or seek reassurance from the teacher. Every request for help should be treated seriously, but without encouraging dependence or 'helplessness' in the girl. This is not easy, but can often be achieved by formulating questions relating to earlier knowledge or to their common experience (remembering they are girls!), thereby boosting confidence.

Encouragement of mastery, not helplessness

Because they themselves are so familiar with science concepts, specialist teachers often do not spend enough time over the introduction of new ideas nor show how they differ from, or relate to, ideas already covered, so that the initial confusion that pupils experience with a new topic may be made worse. If they recognize that this is so, teachers may take steps to improve presentation, but the problem for pupils of moving from one new concept to another in science with its recurrent sense of insecurity and incompetence, remains. Girls' low evaluation of themselves causes them to retreat. Teachers should not accept this but should encourage them positively to face initial confusion or failure to understand, so that they are helped to work successfully in these subjects, and to *expect* to do so.

Positive action

Every opportunity should be taken to provide girls with extra experience in using tools and unfamiliar equipment. Preparation for a display or an open day or some other ploy can be used to overcome their initial diffidence. At secondary school, with co-operation from technicians, girls may be encouraged to help care for apparatus, to assist in putting it out, collecting and checking it in and even carrying out simple repairs. In one school, the author observed third-year girls in an 'activity' period using electrical soldering irons to dismantle components in broken 'lab-packs'; others were collecting and classifying the bits as they were detached. In these ways the girls are made to feel more important and given a stake in the science department, while their self-esteem is raised by developing competence in handling tools and equipment.

Mixed class groupings

The relative advantage of the use of single-sex or mixed groupings within a class is unclear. Young adolescents almost always choose to work in separate sex groups within a mixed class. To require them to do otherwise invites rebellion or a sullen acquiescence, with less work achieved. There is a considerable gap in average maturation level between girls and boys in the twelve to fourteen years range. It may be wiser, therefore, to allow them to work in the same sex groups, but to avoid placing them in any way in competitive roles.

Tackling 'minority' problems

Teachers need to be sensitively aware of the problems facing girls who may be present in small numbers in largely male classes. They must find ways of involving them fully in the work of the class without creating situations which make them feel vulnerable and exposed. Teacher-directed, whole-class questioning may not be the most appropriate way of sorting out ideas. An alternative method might involve small group discussion of prepared stimulus material (during which the teacher is able to interact in a less public way with groups) followed by a reporting session to which the girls, made confident by preparation, may make an appropriate contribution.

Contrary to common assumptions, and in spite of their lack of experience with technical things, girls clearly enjoy practical work in science, and this should therefore form an important part of courses designed to involve girls more fully. It goes without saying that such activities should be adequately managed to prevent disruptive behaviour, for this may provide opportunities for the expression of antagonism between boys and girls. The teacher should not allow sexist comments to pass unchecked, nor be seen to align with one sex against the other.

Monitoring interaction with girls and boys

In their relationship with a mixed class, teachers need to be aware of any bias of attention to, or any type of interaction with, one sex or the other. This is not easy to monitor alone, but the use of a tape recorder, a video camera or a colleague to record interactions, can give valuable feedback. The author has observed many physical science classes in which the boys sit at the front benches, with girls at the rear. This means that teachers are interacting more personally with the boys while giving instructions from the front for practical work or teaching with the use of blackboard or overhead projector. The boys at the front tend to carry on discussion with the teacher, their comments frequently not reaching the back, while the girls sit passively or turn to each other with questions. Even if those sitting at the back benches are brought to the front for this kind of work, they are placed at the sides and are seldom the main focus of the teacher's attention. When practical work is taking place most science teachers circulate well round the groups, but almost invariably come to rest at the front (teacher territory) so that the groups there have greater access to them.

Presentation

In the presentation of subject matter teachers have considerable choice, even within a prescribed examination or departmental syllabus. When choosing examples to illustrate principles, they should relate to girls' common experiences as well as to those of boys. But even here sensitivity needs to be exercised: one must work through differing interests and experiences without confirming limiting stereotypes of behaviour for either sex. Wherever possible, common interests should be used. The GIST project found that both girls and boys would like to know more about how a record player works, but neither sex was interested in a vacuum sweeper![98] In a West German study, when topics were presented as 'sound' and 'light', boys reported greater interest than did girls, but 'hearing' and 'seeing' attracted both equally.[99] So the *context* in which a topic is presented may make all the difference in motivating girls but, at the same time, avoid disadvantaging boys.

Social issues

The greater concern that girls express for social issues should be utilized, for few would deny the importance of such considerations also in the education of boys. The HMI described a single lesson[100] in which pupils investigated the properties of sulphur dioxide in the context of the polluting effects of burning fossil fuels. Girls and boys were equally involved. An example of a flow sheet of work which might develop from the issue of lead in petrol is shown in Figure 6.[101] The rectangular boxes indicate conventional, laboratory-based science which could be included in the topic or extended from it.

An indication of the way in which the 'energy crisis' might be used to establish an understanding of basic thermodynamics is provided in an article by J. Solomon.[102] Further discussions of 'science and society studies in the school curriculum' may be found in another article by her.[103]

Courses built up of such units would differ in several respects from conventional ones. The coming to grips with the issue, its impact on society and its attendant problems for which solutions may or may not be forthcoming, would be a chief objective of the unit, but each would provide opportunities to develop, or consider again, descriptive,

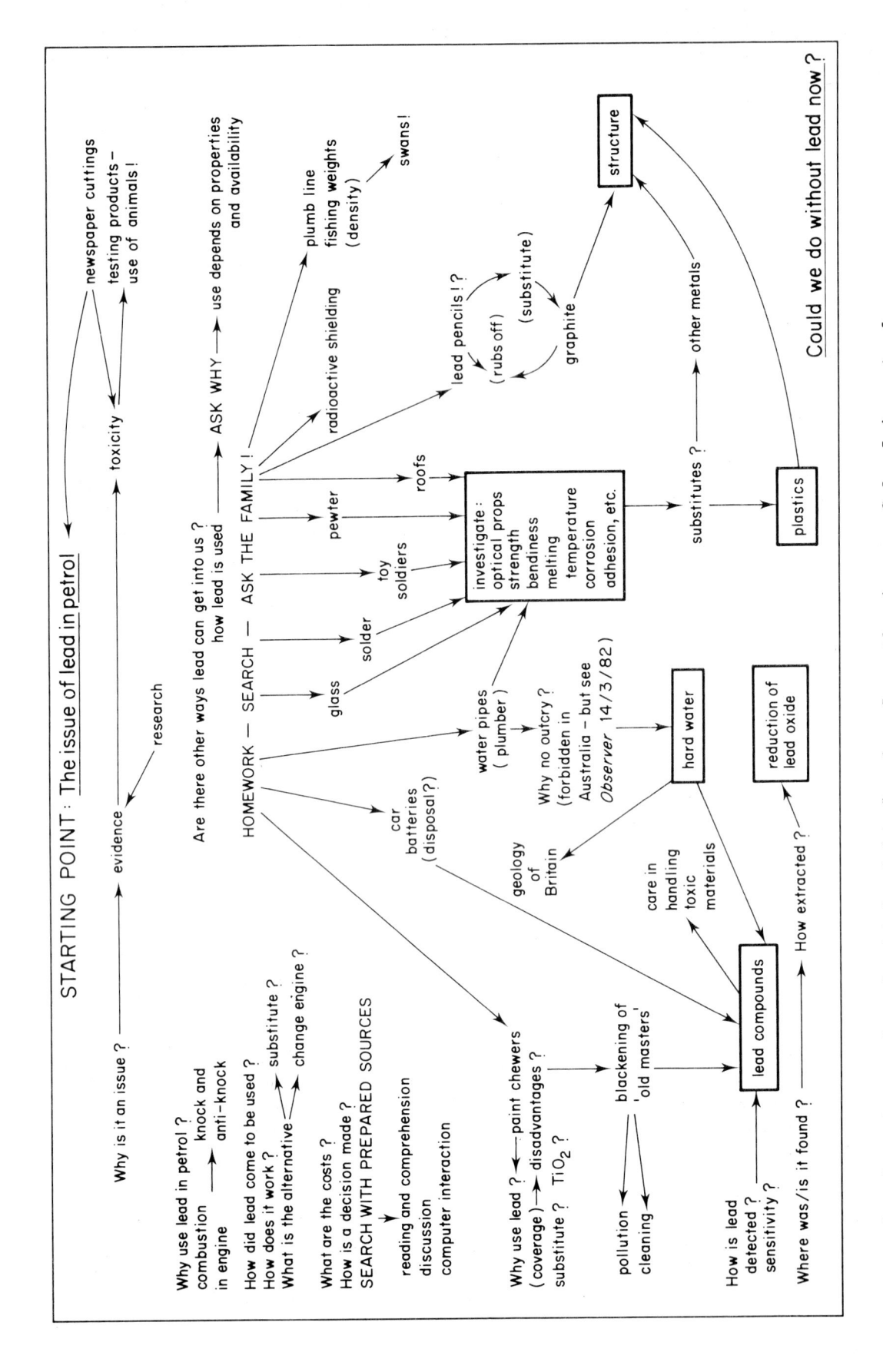

Figure 6 Flow sheet of work which might develop from the issue of lead in petrol

observational aspects of science and associated concepts. Such a
course would not appear as logical or as 'tidy' as courses which derive
their structure from the subject, but it might match more closely to
the way children learn, providing motivation for girls as well as for
boys and frequent visits to ideas for review, extension and consoli-
dation. Thoughtful adolescents, both boys and girls, are likely to be
more attracted to a course of this kind than to the more abstract,
concept-based courses presently offered in schools.

Text and illustrations

Publishers of educational materials have been slow to respond to the
implications of equality of opportunity. The Girls and Physical
Science sub-committee of the Association for Science Education has
prepared guidelines for those designing and publishing materials for
use in schools, to avoid sex-bias. Meanwhile, teachers have to use
materials which are either very impersonal in presentation, or which
include many more references, in text and illustration, to the male.
They may counteract this in several ways: by drawing attention to the
bias and using it as a basis for discussion, by displaying recently-
produced materials showing women working in science,[104] by producing
their own materials in which girls and women feature as often as boys
and men.

Unfortunately many of the situations that amuse us are based on
stereotypes. The use of humour or cartoon images enliven materials,
but care must be taken that sex-stereotypes are not evoked or reinforced
in so doing.

The author is currently preparing pilot materials for a project
which aims to show women and men working at various levels in aspects
of science and technology which relate to topics normally included
in the 11-14 curriculum. The aims are to personalise science, to show
a range of opportunities for work within it and to reduce sex-stereotyping of occupations.

Assessment

The powerful effect of success or failure in tests given by the teacher
during a course, on the motivation and self-image of the pupil should
be recognized. A range of techniques of assessment should be used to
provide feedback to both pupils and teacher of their achievements.
Multiple choice (objective) type tests and essay questions which give
a marked advantage to one sex or the other should be used sparingly
and pupils should be encouraged to see failure as the need to use
different strategies for learning, not as the signal to give up.

Action at school level: primary stage

Patterns of learning in primary schools[105]

Patterns of working in formal education are often established in
primary schools, as are self-images of the pupil as a learner. These
schools need to be sensitively aware of differential feedback to boys
and girls that may result in dependence on the teacher and learned
'helplessness' in the girls. Both girls and boys should be encouraged

to develop a mastery approach to learning. Docile behaviour on the
part of girls should be considered as much a problem in learning as
is over-activity or disruptive behaviour in boys. Working parties or
other in-service strategies could be initiated so that schools may
question their performance in this area and devise alternative ways of
working where necessary.

Involvement in craft/science activities in primary schools

When science- or craft-based activities take place in primary schools,
care should be taken to ensure that both sexes are enabled to participate equally in the range of activities offered. This should cover
the making of models, manipulating apparatus, cooking, clearing up,
making toys in various media, sewing puppets, etc. Both boys and
girls should be encouraged to act in various roles that frequently
emerge in group work: as organizer, scribe, experimenter, reader and
'dogsbody'.

Action at school level: secondary stage

Equality of opportunity

The governors, headteacher and teaching staff of each secondary school
should question the record that the school possesses in enabling
equality of educational opportunities for girls and boys.

Where separate girls' and boys' schools co-exist, assumptions
about the curriculum should be checked, questioning in what ways (and
why) the curriculum would differ if the intake of the schools were
changed overnight to children of the opposite sex. In these schools
the vexed questions of design and technology and home economics remain.
In the context of this pamphlet, concern is for girls' education in
the former. A question of priority at the present time is to investigate how the objectives of design and technology may be achieved
through other established areas of the curriculum in girls' schools.

In co-educational schools, the issue of equal opportunity is ever-present. Ormerod and Duckworth[106] have shown that sex-stereotyping of
subject choice becomes more pronounced than in single-sex schools even
among the most able group of pupils in these schools. CSE statistics
suggest that the bias is more severe with average or less able pupils.
Many schools would claim that girls and boys are treated equally, yet
detailed observation may show that deep-seated assumptions about the
appropriate behaviour for each sex may operate and never be questioned.
Those in positions of leadership in schools should establish some kind
of framework in which such assumptions may be detected, challenged
and reconsidered. This might take one of several forms: a sub-committee which assumes responsibility for monitoring the attitudes,
choices and achievements of girls and boys in the most sex-stereotyped areas of the curriculum, a working party which seeks to discover
ways of changing attitudes, or a training day in which various aspects
of the problem are considered. If an atmosphere of trust can be
established in a school, so that teachers feel able to observe each
other teaching, it may be possible for them to identify classroom
interactions that help or hinder girls' achievement in science classes.
This pamphlet does not recommend the return to single-sex schooling,

but recognizes that schools may wish to make use of teaching in single-sex groups as part of their own enquiry into identified underachievement. What is important is that the issue of equality of opportunity be recognized as problematic and that some whole-school action be taken to attempt to create solutions.

The option system

Recognition was made earlier that the existing diversity in the curriculum in the fourth and fifth years of secondary schooling, although providing the context for pupils to choose according to interests and needs, creates problems of balance for many. In addition, a school often has to compromise between the needs of pupils and the constraints of staffing and accommodation. Where the latter is seen to conflict with the educational needs of children, the school should make strong and continuing representations to the local authority through every means in its power.

In spite of the acknowledged problems schools experience in providing choice for their pupils, they should examine the framing of their option system to determine if it conveys stereotyped expectations of boys and girls. If assumptions about the preferences of girls and boys or their traditional patterns of behaviour and employment are built into the structure of the option system of a school, this will constrain the choices pupils make and reinforce traditional patterns of behaviour. If physics, for example, is 'setted' against French in one block and against home economics in another, few girls will choose physics, although boys will do so in large numbers.

The science area of the curriculum is particularly problematic at the present time. Schools should engage seriously in the debate about core sciences and how this might prepare all young people both for 'living' and for employment, by providing a foundation from which knowledge can expand informally and from which further qualifications in any area of science may be acquired. No science course in the early years of tertiary education (i.e. post 16+) should be inaccessible to an individual as a result of choices made at fourteen years.

Guidance and counselling

The current position of choice among many options demands the sensitive counselling of pupils. The 'one-off' explanation of the implications of the option system is not enough. The adolescent years are a time when young people need help in developing their own identity as they move from dependence to maturity. Guidance and counselling provides an essential support throughout this time.

The purpose and function of each part of the curriculum should be made clear to young people. The ways in which present study may expand into adult life (in employment, discharging civic responsibilities, in caring for themselves and others, or in leisure) should be conveyed to pupils as part of their work in schools. Their own current interests frequently provide motivation tapped by good teaching, but at the same time they should be encouraged to anticipate future needs.

43

In particular, the patterns of employment already undertaken by women in our society should be presented clearly to girls, with discussion of rewards, frustrations and possible future developments as employment patterns change. A time of choice, such as occurs at fourteen years, needs to be preceded by an extensive period of information-gathering, reflection and consultation.

The tape/slide sequence, advising pupils of the contribution that physics and chemistry can make to participation in various fields of employment, was an attempt to provide this. The strategy of its use was a particularly effective one in the original context. The Girls and Physical Science sub-committee of ASE has enabled multiple copies of this package to be made available through a grant from the Department of Industry.* Teachers may, however, wish to develop their own material.

It is recommended that something like this tape/slide sequence form part of the science department resources in every school and be used by its members, in science lessons, some weeks before pupils have to make choices which may irrevocably exclude them from physical science, as in the present system.

Links with industry and commerce

Many schools are currently establishing links with local industry and commerce, some through the link schemes set up initially by the chemical industry, at the end of the 1960s, some through work-experience placements for the fourteen-to-sixteen age groups, others through recent projects such as the CBI Understanding British Industry (UBI) Project or the Schools Council Industry Project. These links are potential vehicles through which problems relating to girls' entry to non-technical areas of work could be identified and solutions sought, and girls could be made aware of existing opportunities for such work. E. Byrne[107] reported that, where a school had a deliberate policy of giving girls experience of work that was traditionally male dominated, more girls went on to enter career-based or technical further education from this school than from others in the same area.

Local links may also be used to invite personnel from various levels of employment into the school, during the extended guidance and counselling programme, to talk to pupils about the work they do. Within this context it would be possible to ask firms to identify women working in non-traditional jobs and arrange for them, where appropriate, to present this area of working to pupils.† For both girls and boys to become aware of women working in these jobs would serve to break down stereotypes of 'appropriate' behaviour for both sexes. Information about girls from the school who have moved on to work in traditional male areas should be made available to young children in booklets, wall displays or in some other way. The

---

* They may be borrowed from a local Science and Technology Regional Organisation (SATRO) or purchased from the Headquarters of Association for Science Education, College Lane, Hatfield.

† The GIST project, based at Manchester Polytechnic, has developed such an arrangement: the VISTA project.

responsibility for this should rest with the careers teacher.

Remedial or compensatory programmes

In language work, where boys experience more difficulty than girls do, remedial work is well established. In mathematics and physical science, where girls (for whatever reason) have more problems than boys, there is little or no tradition of compensatory work. Perhaps abilities in these areas are assumed to be more innate. Or it may be that the practice of setting in mathematics nullifies the concept of 'remedial'. It is only recently that girls' lack of experience with three-dimensional constructional toys or those involving electric motors or mechanical moving parts has been seen to disadvantage them in the laboratory. It should be possible to provide compensatory experience for girls. This could be achieved through varied projects such as model theatre work, or the making of toys for a local children's home.

The kind of 'clinic' that HMI report[108] would provide older girls with the opportunity to ask for help in a less daunting atmosphere than they find in a mainly male class. The setting up of such clinics would reinforce the schools' concern and caring role to the pupils and provide teachers with an opportunity to talk through concepts with individual pupils - opportunities not often presented in the demanding context of class teaching. They would, of course, add to a teacher's day, but many science teachers would welcome the formalizing of a practice they already carry out. The advantage of a formal arrangement is that it removes the embarrassment many girls feel in approaching a male member of staff for extra attention.

The science curriculum

While choice among the three sciences remains in the option system, science departments should take seriously the HMI[109] criticism of the marked change in the presentation of work in physics and chemistry in year three where it becomes more abstract, conceptual, mathematical, less practical and divorced from everyday life - all changes which appear to discourage girls more than boys. The change to more advanced working should be made more gradually. Practical work and the relevance of topics to the life of the pupil should be retained. If teachers feel strongly that the examination syllabus does not allow the time to do this, then strong recommendations should be made to examining boards to change syllabuses. There is a gathering consensus that physics and chemistry syllabuses should be pruned. Teachers' representatives have considerable weight on examining boards. They should organize themselves to effect changes.

Science departments should scrutinize all printed or duplicated materials used in teaching. If any present science through a masculine stereotype, they should be rejected (if dispensable), modified (if possible) or compensated for (if their use is unavoidable). Strong protests should be made to publishers of any material conveying sex-role stereotypes.

Action at LEA level

The equal opportunity debate and girls' science education

The local education authority has a responsibility to monitor equal opportunities in education for girls and boys and to ensure that it is provided. There is ample evidence that girls are ill-prepared by their education in science to take advantage of training or employment opportunities, nor are many aware of the opportunities that are available.

There is need for initiatives to be taken both in the provision of more extensive and informative careers education and in reducing sex-stereotyped expectations of young people. LEA careers advisers should take the lead in this and ensure that all careers teachers in the schools for which they have responsibility have adequate information, effective training and the appropriate orientation to perform the delegated careers work in these schools.

Science advisers are influential in raising questions and highlighting issues within the schools in their authority. Several have recognized the disadvantage to girls of their present pattern of science education and have organized meetings in which this has been discussed. Ideally such meetings should be followed up by working parties within the authority so that real changes may be effected in the schools.

This work in careers and in science education should be firmly based in a framework in which the reality of equal provision and equal opportunities for boys and girls may be questioned and monitored. Some LEAs have created a special post with responsibility for this. There is value in such a post, but only if its creation involves an intention to bring about change, not a discharge of responsibility.

Science in primary schools

Very little of the earlier discussion has been focused on the primary school. One reason for this is that very little research has been conducted into differences in the science programme for boys and girls at the primary stage. HMI's survey of primary schools[110] highlights the inadequate provision for science education in most schools. This is a direct consequence of the alienation from science of most of the young women who form the greatest part of the teaching force at the primary stage. There is an urgent need for continuing and long-term in-service support for these teachers to enable them to expand this area of the curriculum. The Inspectors, reporting on girls' science education,[111] found evidence of good primary school experience overcoming girls' feelings of strangeness in science work in the secondary school.

Provision for practical subjects in secondary schools

Each local education authority carries responsibility for the educational provision in its area. Facilities for science education have improved dramatically in secondary schools in many areas as a consequence of comprehensive reorganization. But the level of staffing and accommodation in science caters only for the demand of the present. We have seen the HMI judge these to be inadequate in many places (but even 'acceptable' levels have been fixed on the assumption that few girls will continue with the study of the physical sciences and technology). They suggest that falling rolls may alleviate the position to some extent. This will not be the case, however, if the response of local authorities is to close schools, with the subsequent loss of accommodation. If the present central government financial constraints continue, local authorities will be hard-pressed to meet the level of provision required by an expansion of girls' participation in practical subjects. Education committees should initiate and sustain a lobby to ensure that adequate facilities in these areas are available to both girls and boys.

Girls into local employment at 16+ and 18+

If schools *are* successful in encouraging girls to develop skills enabling them to do work hitherto largely performed by men, then local employers must be prepared seriously to consider applications from girls for such work. This could be facilitated through links currently being established between schools and local industry and commerce.

Girls who break new ground in this way may feel lonely and isolated but, at the same time, the focus of much (sometimes hostile) attention. Firms employing them may be at a loss to know how to tackle problems arising within the work force. The YWCA is currently developing training courses (in response to a request from an employer in this position) which are designed to help girls, and those with whom they work, to adjust to the novel situation. This work is being extended by a DES grant. Such training courses might be initiated within the Further Education Section for the sixteen-to-nineteen age group.

The LEA careers adviser is well-placed to promote the setting up of a network of women employed at various levels in local industry and commerce. This local organization could then be used to advise girls in schools and to support those who attempt to follow them. The GIST project[112] describes how women have been used in this way in project schools. An EOC-sponsored piece of research in the north of England[113] shows the active discouragement faced by girls, at present, who aspire to non-traditional areas of work on leaving school.

Action at the national level

Common core and options

The option system presently covering work in the last two years of compulsory schooling has evolved from changes in the organization of both the public examination system (from a grouped subject examination to one of single subject entry) and of secondary schools (to provide for the full range of ability) - both considered by many to be reforms in themselves. But the resulting system of choice among many options now works to the disadvantage of a large number of children who complete their schooling in no way equipped for life in the late twentieth century. The debate on the objectives of secondary education and the question of a common core of subjects should be pursued vigorously to identify and attempt to instil the skills young people need to acquire through their formal education.

Science – core or options

'Science for all' is becoming a more universally accepted objective. The Association for Science Education is committed to it, but is debating what form it should take;[114] the Secretaries of State for Education and for Wales propose it,[115] and HMI state that 'Science for all, to include physical sciences, should be the ultimate goal'.[116]

A major initiative in seeking to establish operational definitions of 'Science for all' is the Secondary Science Curriculum Review established in September 1981 by the DES, the Schools Council and the Association for Science Education. This is a five-year programme of research and development which focuses on the form and content of the science curriculum for all young people aged eleven to sixteen years. The programme operates at two levels and involves a number of teacher-based working groups and development teams designing and evaluating a range of different approaches to 'Science for all'. At the same time a central co-ordinating group is negotiating acceptance of curricular alternatives at the national level with higher and further education, industry, professional organizations and examination boards. Whilst the Review is concerned with the science education of pupils of all abilities, specific attention is being given to the particular aspirations of girls. A final major objective of the Review is that of seeking to establish more effective ways of co-ordinating science-based, or science-related, activities across the secondary school curriculum. This will involve a careful examination of the aims of science education in the context of secondary education for all.

But we are faced with the dilemma of three separate sciences. Under the present 'examination-subject-slot' these take up an unwarranted slice of the curriculum, leading, as was argued in Chapter 3, to an unbalanced curriculum if all are chosen or a distorted science experience if one or more are rejected.

The pressures at present acting on and in schools are decreasing the numbers of able children following broad-based courses in science. This has much to do with teachers' interpretation of demands made by employers, parents and tertiary education institutions, but also with the pleasure that specialist teachers experience in teaching their own subject and the identity this creates for them. In this context, it is unrealistic to make recommendations to the schools for broad-based courses and expect change to occur. Discussions should take place at national level, to include the Schools Council, DES, universities and CNAA, employers, professional organizations, teachers' organizations and other bodies who contribute to pressure on schools so that any change regarded as desirable may be facilitated.

Integration in the curriculum

Experiments to integrate aspects of the study of home economics, design and technology and science – all establishing survival skills for living in our present society – should be encouraged.

Science examinations

The weight of evidence identifying the greater difficulty that young people experience in achieving success in the physical sciences compared to other areas of the curriculum should no longer be ignored.

The supply of teachers

The provision of teachers of mathematics, physical sciences and design and technology has been problematic for many years. The recent piloting of scholarships for well-qualified graduates of mathematics and physics who are prepared to enter teacher training may be a first step to improving the supply of teachers in these subjects. The position in design and technology is more complex. The low status that 'craft' subjects have assumed in most comprehensive schools has been disturbed only a little by the conversion to 'design and technology' with wider educational objectives. The outcome is that few young people of ability continue with the subject in later years of schooling and few achieve the two A-level subject passes required for entry to teacher education courses. Urgent steps should be taken at national level to improve the status of this curriculum area, and to extend to all pupils the chance to develop the broad skills of problem-solving and decision-making that it can offer.

If girls continue in larger numbers with the study of mathematics, physical science and technology, the pool from which graduates may be attracted to teaching will be increased. However, central government must recognize that to accommodate girls adequately in these subjects an expansion not only of staffing, but of facilities, may be necessary.

REFERENCES

Chapter 1

1. Department of Education and Science, *Enquiry into the Flow of Candidates in Science and Technology into Higher Education* [The Dainton Report]. HMSO, 1968.

2. In this project materials were developed in the 1960s for pupils and teachers in the specialist sciences (GCE O and A level), in integrated science (Nuffield Secondary Science), and for primary schools (Nuffield Junior Science). They are available, some now in revised form, from Longman.

3. Department of Educaton and Science, *Aspects of Secondary Education in England*, a survey by HM Inspectors of Schools. HMSO, 1979.

4. Ibid, p.265.

5. E. Byrne. 'Inequality in education - discriminal resource - allocation in schools?' in R. Meighan and J. Doherty (eds.). *Education and Sex Roles*, special issue of *Educational Review*, vol.27, 1975, no.3, pp.179-191.

6. J. Brierley. 'Sex differences in education', *Trends in Education*, January 1975.

7. Equal Opportunities Commission. *The Fact about Women is...* EOC, 1982.

8. Ibid.

9. I. Rauta and A. Hunt. *Fifth Form Girls: Their Hopes for the Future.* HMSO, 1975.

10. Irene C. Peden. 'The missing half of our technical potential: can we motivate the girls?', *Mathematics Teacher*, vol.58, January 1965, pp.2-13.

11. Equal Opportunities Commission, 1982 (see note 7).

12. E. Bird. *Information and Technology in the Office: The Impact on Women's Jobs.* Equal Opportunities Commission, 1980.

13. J.P. Ward. 'Adolescent girls and modes of knowledge' in R. Meighan and J. Doherty (eds.). *Education and Sex Roles*, special issue of *Educational Review*, vol.27, 1975, no.3, pp.221-228.

14. *Schools Council Science 5-13 Project materials* are published by Macdonald Education.

Chapter 2

15. L. Comber and J. Keeves. *Science Education in Nineteen Countries*. Halstead Press, 1973.

16. A. Kelly. *Girls and Science*, IEA Monograph Studies No. 9. Almquist and Wiksell International, 1978.

17. A. Kelly (ed.). *The Missing Half: Girls and Science Education*. Manchester University Press, 1981.

18. Department of Education and Science. *Girls and Science*, HMI Series: Matters for Discussion 13. HMSO, 1980.

19. DES, 1979 (see note 3).

20. Ibid, p.169.

21. A.B. Stillman. 'The rationale for abilities testing', *School Science Review*, vol.63, 1982, no.224, pp.423-433.

22. Kelly, 1978 (see note 16).

23. e.g. see A. Patterson, 'You want physics for everything'. *Education in Science*, April 1980.

24. A. Kelly. 'Women in science: a bibliographic review', *Durham Research Review*, vol.7, spring 1976.

25. M. Eddowes. *Humble Pi: The Mathematics Education of Girls*. Schools Council Programme Pamphlet. Longman, York, 1983.

26. S. Smith. 'Should they be kept apart?', *Times Educational Supplement*, 18 July 1980.

27. E. Maccoby and C. Jacklin. *The Psychology of Sex Differences*. Wiley, 1975.

28. B. Smail, J. Whyte and A. Kelly. 'Girls into science and technology: the first two years'. Paper submitted at the Girls and Science and Technology Conference, Eindhoven, Holland, November 1981.

29. C. Dweck. 'Learned helplessness or taught helplessness?'. Paper presented at Sex Differentiation in Schooling Conference, Churchill College, Cambridge, 1980.

30. J.S. Hyde. 'How large are cognitive gender differences?', *American Psychologist*, vol.36, 1981, no.8.

31. J.S. King. 'Sex differences and careers guidance', *Careers Bulletin*, Department of Employment Careers Services Branch, spring 1976.

32. Statement made by Dr Barbara Lloyd of Sussex University in a programme on 'The Sexes' broadcast in the autumn of 1980 on BBC Radio 4.

33. Stillman, 1982 (see note 21).

34. J. Head. 'Personality and the pursuit of science', *Studies in Science Education*, vol.6, 1979.

35. J. Head. 'A model to link personality characteristics to a preference for science', *European Journal of Science Education*, vol.2, 1980, pp.295-300.

36. J. Head and M. Shayer. 'Loevinger's ego development measures - a new research tool?', *British Educational Research Journal*, vol.6, 1980, pp.21-27.

37. A. Smithers and J. Collings. 'Girls studying science in the sixth form' in A. Kelly (ed.). *The Missing Half*. Manchester University Press, 1981.

38. Head, 1980 (see note 35).

39. DES, 1980 (see note 18), pp.22-23.

40. *What's a girl like you...?*, available from the Central Film Library, Central Office of Information, Hercules Road, London SE7 AC1, as film or videotape.

41. Publicity Section, Equal Opportunities Commission, Overseas House, Quay Street, Manchester M3 3HN.

42. Careers Research and Advisory Centre. *Women in Industry*. Hobson's Press, Cambridge, 1981. General Electric Company. *Women in Research in GEC*. Available from 1 Stanhope Gate, London W1A 1EH.

43. G. Walford. 'Sex bias in physics textbooks', *School Science Review*, vol.62, 1980, no.219.

44. R.R. Dale. *Mixed or Single-sex Schools?*, vol.3. Routledge and Kegan Paul, 1974.

45. R. Wood and C. Ferguson. 'Unproven case for coeducation', *Times Educational Supplement*, 4 October 1974.

46. J. Harding. 'Sex differences in examination performance at 16+', *Physics Education*, Institute of Physics, vol.14, July 1979. Also J. Harding, 'Sex differences in science examinations' in A. Kelly (ed.). *The Missing Half*. Manchester University Press, 1981.

47. Harding, 1979 (see note 46).

48. J. Newsom. *The Education of Girls*. Faber & Faber, 1948.
    J. Newsom. *Half our Future*. HMSO, 1963.

49. DES, 1980 (see note 18).

50. DES, 1979 (see note 3).

51. DES, 1980 (see note 18), p.27.

52. Byrne, 1975 (see note 5).

53. For example: S. Sharpe. *Just Like a Girl*. Penguin, 1976. E.G. Belotti. *Little Girls*. Writers and Readers Publishing Co-operative, 1975. E. Byrne. *Women and Education*. Tavistock Publications, 1978.

54. Lloyd, 1980 (see note 32).

55. Byrne, 1978 (see note 53).

56. P. Torrance. 'Changing reactions of pre-adolescent girls to science tasks' in *Education and the Creative Potential*. Minnesota University Press, 1963.

57. J. Walberg. 'Dimensions of scientific interests in boys and girls studying physics', *Science Education*, vol.51, 1967, no.2, pp.111-116.

58. DES, 1979 (see note 3), pp.166-167.

59. DES, 1980 (see note 18), p.22.

60. Comments made when discussing the use of new science curricula in 1972/73 as part of the Curriculum Diffusion Research Project, based at Chelsea College.

61. DES, 1980 (see note 18), p.16.

62. Kelly, 1976 (see note 24).

63. Ibid, p.262.

64. D. Ebbutt. 'Girls' science: boys' science revisited' in A. Kelly (ed.). *The Missing Half*. Manchester University Press, 1981, pp.211, 213.

65. DES, 1980 (see note 18), pp.20-21.

66. M.B. Ormerod. 'Factors differentially affecting the science option preferences, choices and attitudes of boys and girls' in A. Kelly (ed.). *The Missing Half*. Manchester University Press, 1981.

67. M.B. Ormerod and D. Duckworth. *Pupils' Attitudes to Science*. NFER Publishing, 1975.

68. Head, 1980 (see note 35).

69. DES, 1980 (see note 18), pp.7 and 25.

70. J. Eggleston, M. Galton and M. Jones. *Processes and Products of Science Teaching*, Schools Council Research Studies. Macmillan Education, 1976.

71. M. Galton. 'Differential treatment of boy and girl, during science lessons' in A. Kelly (ed.). *The Missing Half*. Manchester University Press, 1981.

72. Kelly, 1981 (see note 17).

73. DES, 1980 (see note 18), p.118.

74. Kelly, 1981 (see note 17), and DES, 1980 (see note 18).

75. Kelly, 1981 (see note 17), pp.233 and 243-245.

76. DES, 1980 (see note 18), pp.20, 24 and 25.

77. T. Blackstone. 'The education of girls today' in J. Mitchell and A. Oakley (eds.). *The Rights and Wrongs of Women*. Penguin, 1976.

78. DES, 1980 (see note 18), p.10, and Kelly, 1981 (see note 17), p.235.

79. Kelly, 1981 (see note 17), p.234.

80. DES, 1979 (see note 3), and 1980 (see note 18).

81. DES, 1980 (see note 18), pp.32-33.

82. Ormerod and Duckworth, 1975 (see note 67).

83. Harding, 1979 and 1981 (see note 46).

84. C. Ferguson. Unpublished report, School Examinations Department, University of London.

85. R.J.L. Murphy. 'Sex differences in objective test performance'. Paper presented at the British Educational Research Association Conference, 1981.

86. Harding, 1979 (see note 46).

87. 'Multiple-choice under fire. Report from US'. *Times Educational Supplement*, 27 November 1981.

88. I.V.S. Mullis. 'Educational achievement and sex discrimination'. Unpublished report, National Assessment of Educational Progress (USA), 1975.

89. J. Harding. 'Sex-stereotyping: power and control'. Oxford Science Education Conference Report, 1981. Available from Department of Educational Studies, Norham Gardens, Oxford.

90. DES, 1979 (see note 3), p.25.

91. DES, 1980 (see note 18), p.12.

92. Kelly, 1981 (see note 17), p.135.

93. D. Ebbutt. 'Science options in a girls' grammar school' in A. Kelly (ed.). *The Missing Half*. Manchester University Press, 1981.

94. M. Reid. *A Matter of Choice*. NFER Publishing, 1974. DES, 1980 (see note 18).

95. M. Hearn. 'Girls for physical science', *Education in Science*, April 1979.

96. Patterson, 1980 (see note 23).

97. C. McPherson. 'Science choices', correspondence page, *Education in Science*, November 1980.

Chapter 3

98. Smail *et al.*, 1981 (see note 28).

99. L. Hoffman. 'Consequences for science education based on the results of girls' learning interests'. Girls and Science and Technology Conference, Eindhoven, Holland, November 1981, vol.2 contributions.

100. DES, 1980 (see note 18), pp.24 and 25.

101. J. Head has included this topic in a contribution to the *Handbook for Pupils*, Nuffield Revised O level Chemistry, Chapter 12 'Man, chemistry and society'. At Chelsea College, student teachers involved in a short course with N. Ryder in 1981, 'Science in political and social issues', developed a resource pack for teachers around the issue of lead in petrol. Figure 6 is the flow sheet for a module in a curriculum project, 'Chemistry from issues', being developed at Chelsea College, Centre for Science and Mathematics Education, with PGCE students, 1982/83.

102. J. Solomon. 'How children learn about energy', *School Science Review*, vol.63, 1982, no.224, pp.415-422.

103. J. Solomon. 'Science and society studies in the school curriculum', *School Science Review*, vol.62, 1980, no.219, pp.213-219.

104. Such as posters produced by the EOC depicting women scientists, Engineering Industries Training Board careers materials, etc.

105. See a forthcoming pamphlet in this series by J. Whyte. *Beyond the Wendy House: Sex Role Stereotyping in Primary Schools*. Schools Council Programme Pamphlet. Longman, York, 1983.

106. Ormerod and Duckworth, 1975 (see note 67).

107. Byrne, 1975 (see note 5).

108. DES, 1980 (see note 18).

109. Ibid.

110. Department of Education and Science. *Primary Education in England*, a survey by HM Inspectors of Schools. HMSO, 1978.

111. DES, 1980 (see note 18).

112. Smail *et al.*, 1981 (see note 28).

113. Equal Opportunities Commission. *Side-tracked*. EOC, 1981.

114. Association for Science Education. *Alternatives for Science Education: A Consultative Document*. ASE, 1979. Association for Science Education. *Education through Science: Policy Statement*. ASE, 1981.

115. Department of Education and Science. *A Framework for the School Curriculum:* Proposals for consultation by the Secretaries of State for Education and Science and for Wales. DES, 1980. Department of Education and Science. *Science Education in Schools*, a consultative document. DES, 1982.

116. DES, 1980 (see note 18).